ROOTS

Published in 2021 by Hardie Grant Books, an imprint of Hardie Grant Publishing

Hardie Grant Books (Melbourne)
Wurundjeri Country
Building 1, 658 Church Street
Richmond, Victoria 3121

Hardie Grant Books (London)
5th & 6th Floors
52–54 Southwark Street London SE1 1UN

hardiegrantbooks.com

 A catalogue record for this
book is available from the
National Library of Australia

Roots
ISBN 978 1 74379 781 5

10 9 8 7 6 5 4 3 2 1

Cover and text design by Mietta Yans
Typeset in 12.5/18 pt Garamond by Post Pre-Press Group
Printed in Australia by Griffin Press, part of Ovato, an Accredited ISO AS/NZS 14001
Environmental Management System printer

 The paper this book is printed on is certified against the Forest
Stewardship Council® Standards. Griffin Press holds FSC® chain
of custody certification SGSHK-COC-005088. FSC® promotes
environmentally responsible, socially beneficial and economically viable
management of the world's forests.

Hardie Grant acknowledges the Traditional Owners of the country on which we work,
the Wurundjeri people of the Kulin nation and the Gadigal people of the Eora nation,
and recognises their continuing connection to the land, waters and culture. We pay our
respects to their Elders past, present and emerging.

ROOTS

HOME IS WHO WE ARE

**Voices from the
SBS Emerging
Writers'
Competition**

Hardie Grant

BOOKS

CONTENTS

FOREWORD

In August 2020, SBS Voices called on bold new writers to share their stories of living and growing up in modern Australia. The inaugural SBS Emerging Writers' Competition attracted massive interest, with more than 2000 entries from all over the country, including dozens of First Nations entrants. What this competition showed was the strength, vitality and brilliance of writers who are mostly working from outside the (so-called) mainstream.

Judges were looking for courageous and original voices, writing with a sharp take on modern Australian life, and nuanced views on our diverse realities. The mix was so powerful and so striking that choosing the shortlist was a real problem. Scores of excellent pieces had to be set aside, many of them of publishable quality, and all of them a stark reminder that Australia is so much more than we are often led to believe. This is a country of blak, brown and yellow voices. It is the country of those who know they don't feature in the mainstream imagination. The country of those excluded, downtrodden and for too long left out of the picture.

In these pages are thirty of the best stories and most exciting voices from the competition. They explore place, era, sexuality, religion, neurodiversity and disability, ethnicity and culture, and the myriad ways you can call Australia home. This is storytelling that requires you to see the world from a different perspective – that brings something new to the conversation. There are fierce blows struck against casual racism, gut-punches of stories offering hard-won wisdom, strength and perspective, insights both hilarious and moving, and words that make you tingle with the recognition that you are reading important new voices in Australian writing.

These voices and their stories are important because if we don't showcase the richness of who we are, it will prevent us from understanding ourselves, our families, our communities, our neighbourhoods and this country. To have conversations about our history and our future, we need this.

– Melissa Lucashenko and Benjamin Law, judges of the 2020 SBS Emerging Writers' Competition

MEDIUM-BEIGE

ALANA HICKS

He pulled up in a beat-up old Honda Civic the colour of congealed blood. A combination of burgundy and rust, a mélange, like me. If I was choosing a foundation, you might think tan, or honey, or light brown, but none are a true match. Turns out the best colour for me is medium-beige, way whiter than I feel. I've always struggled with foundations. What is the right tone to mask my imperfections? How can I disguise myself, cover my breakout melanin? The freckles that hint at the Scottish in my blood, the terracotta of my right arm, the sand of my left. My ghost face. A patchwork of different shades determined by a shifting sun.

The Honda contained a skinny boy-adult with long, scraggly brown hair who stared out the driver's side window like the subject of an old-timey painting. He had an elusive expression, slightly confused. Something made me hold my breath, made me feel like I'd seen the face of my future.

Greer, Scott and I stood in the carpark of the local train station waiting for Scott's dealer. I was fifteen and I smoked pot. A lot. I was more experienced than Greer in the drug department; despite her spiky dog collar, peroxide pixie cut and labret stud, I was the tougher of the two of us. I'd come from a place of deep violence and complex politics, Papua New Guinea. My mother and I were yanked away from that place after a situation that unfolded in the same amount of time that it takes the sun to set in the Pacific. One minute.

The sun had been blazing as we rolled down our street past a group of men, faces alight with the potential for menace. I conducted the ritual of our arrival home, dashing out of the car with its tinted windows to the six-foot barbed-wire fence, unlocking the padlock and widening the gate just enough for my mother to drive through. But as the sun began its descent, I saw the silhouettes moving faster towards me. Instinctually I hid my scrawny ten-year-old self behind a small, leafless tree. I was expert at hiding, at camouflage. I had perfected being invisible. Always look down, don't make a point of your difference, don't be too loud. Don't be too white in the black crowd, don't be too black in the white one. No-one will notice you if you're quiet and pretend to be shy. Blend in. Especially at the jawline.

I watched as they surrounded her car, banging on the windows, screaming for her to get out. My father, in the house, shouting the opposite, Don't get out. I knew she would get out. I was not in the car with her. She would get out, draw attention away from me, and bear the brunt of whatever was to come. She opened the door a crack, they flung it open. I saw a machete move to her throat,

I knew my only job was to run. Run to the back door, into the kitchen. By now it was pure darkness. My father was no longer in the living room. I picked up the phone and called the cops. I was trained for this.

She wasn't hurt. I wasn't hurt. They took the car, they took her bag. It was empty of kina, only some Aussie dollars she had recently exchanged for my next solo trip to Sydney. I travelled to Sydney most school holidays, stayed with my grandfather, felt an aloneness I didn't feel in Port Moresby. Something about having freedom but nowhere to go, no-one to be free with, made the freedom redundant.

After the incident, my father took to pacing. All the time pacing, up and down. What to do, what to do. My grandfather solved the problem by dying. He left his old weatherboard worker's cottage to my father. And so my mother and I moved, without my much older siblings, without my dad, who stayed for work. Splitting our family forever and migrating like birds to this cobwebby, strange, poo-coloured house, in a very white, very wealthy Sydney suburb where we would stick out the rest of our lives. The rest of our lives, determined by the sinking of a tropical sun.

All this in me as I began to shape myself after moving to Australia. I didn't wear my identity on my T-shirt or face like Greer. I didn't smoke weed to rebel. I smoked to quiet the night terrors. My shaky foundation reverberated in my brain. Made it hard to sleep. To turn my brain off I needed something, and found it. With weed I found other alone-people, others who were trying to suppress a tremor. Grunge music was a place for my detachment, my unease. I related to those sad-sack voices calling for help in long, drawn-out whiny tones. Radiohead made me feel that being abnormal was normal, while Nirvana did the same for sadness. Rage Against the Machine sharpened anger into a weapon.

The Honda turned into the carpark. We walked slowly towards it, Greer and Scott first, me trailing behind. My heart beating in my ears. Something about this boy. Something I couldn't put my finger on.

The something was love, falling arse-first. Like a double jump on a trampoline, he made me unexpectedly high, even without the weed. But he was twenty years old and I was not. I couldn't even drink, but I didn't need to be eighteen to smoke a tonne of pot and forge a connection as his most regular client. After months of pining, and several aborted attempts at forcing a beautiful connection, we were still mostly strangers. Relegated only to interactions based on occasional drug deals. He was a small-time supplier, in it just to smoke his own profits.

One day, after I had finally turned sixteen, I knew what I needed to do. I called his pizza shop, because of course he was a pizza and drug deliverer, and I ordered a Hawaiian. I ordered it as near to closing time as possible, and when he arrived I asked if he wanted to split it with me, maybe have a cone, chill out in my caravan. Yes, I had a sick caravan. The weatherboard mansion couldn't contain my anxiety and, to make me happy, Mum let me have a second-hand caravan in the backyard, decked out in frilly curtains and rash-coloured pink walls. Honda Boy and I ate pizza and kissed with greasy lips. The caravan was a Dutch oven filling with our burgeoning love and weed smoke.

Through Honda Boy I saw teenage white culture, the music

and skating, the casual misogyny, the cruelty of class. I was white enough to be accepted, to have the privilege of not noticing how I was exoticised by this white boy and all the white boys that came after him. One thing he said, the thing I will never forget, caused an earthquake in my Doc Martens. We were sitting in a gutter, I don't recall why. We were always sitting on the street, that's what young people did in the '90s, sit in the gutter, waiting, always waiting, for something. I don't remember the conversation that led to it, but for some reason he blurted, You know, I wouldn't be with you if you looked like your mother.

My blood vessels were like those cars with the stickers on them, making urgent deliveries to different parts of my body. Rushing to my ears, my hands, my feet. Compelling me to get up and abandon whatever this was, and fast. In as long as it takes for a tropical sun to set, I recalled the echoes of the words from the mouths of the boys who wanted a piece of me, on their terms only. You're not Asian, are you? Because I don't date Asians. You look like a boy. Your pussy is too hairy. You're a reject. You have a reject body.

People used the term reject flexibly back then, as an adjective, verb and noun, and sometimes all three at once. Errrrrr reeeeeeeject. These words and their intentions were more baffling than hurtful. My mother endured worse: physical violence, institutionalised exclusion, denial of education, denial of her basic human rights. Words couldn't penetrate the barrier of my shell, *her* experiences hardened *me*. The people who said them were not worth crying over. As she's always said, I know who I am, no-one can take that away.

Fearless.

Honda Boy would have been lucky if my mother looked twice at him. He was afraid of her blackness, and of what it represented to me. I recognised it in a lot of the boys, they wanted a me without my culture, without my mother. They wanted a mask. I tried to cultivate that, but over time masks crack, leaving chasm-like craters in the dead and dying clay.

The Australia of my youth was not diverse. It was medium-beige.

I migrated a second time, from the Hills to the Inner West, where the colour palette increased and poets somehow made money. Here was a different Australia. Everything that came before viewed through a post-millennial telescope, and commonly agreed to be daggy and stupid. Everything was simultaneously much better and much worse. I wound my way through the veins of the city, of the west and greater west, the hills, mountains and beaches. The ovals, the parks, the pubs. Finding beautiful weirdos in their many forms. Each meeting and moment moulding and shaping my clay.

And I know that all over, people wear masks, faded and rusty paint jobs to shield against the extremities of life. I also know I don't give a fuck what shade I need to be to blend in. I only hope I resemble my mother.

SCHISM

NADIA JOHANSEN

Dot, dot, dot, the beige liquid over my brow and across my nose. Work quickly, it will soon dry down to a powder. Look into the eyes of the woman applying it. They're coloured by river water. The water that fills the Maranoa and changes colour with her moods. Today they're the yellow/green/brown of the river at dusk when the sunlight, spread out by the gum leaves, sinks into its muddy depths. They're still, like the river at day's end when a pregnant quiet descends. Holding the beginnings of nocturnal feasting. Waiting for the undercurrent of animal calls and insect scurrying to grow louder as the sun slips down to sleep below the tree line.

The sun is fully awake here in my bathroom. It's streaming through the open window to reflect back at me from every surface. I want to shield my eyes. Maybe draw the blinds and go back to bed. But the woman won't let me. She draws up her chin and rolls back her shoulders so that I'll do the same. Many people fought to get you where you are today. Absence or silence would be a betrayal. Yellow/green/brown eyes bore into mine. Do it for the girl.

Last night

Mum calls me to kill time on her way home from work. I sit on my bed ready to get the latest gossip from back home. As she drives, I hear every noise. The tick, tick, tick of the indicators and the whoosh of other cars.

The girl died by suicide, Mum tells me.

'But she must've been only sixteen,' I say. My sister's age.

'She was fifteen,' Mum sighs, 'and she was so loved.' Tick, tick, tick. My knees go funny and the floor rushes up to hit my backside.

The girl died by suicide last year inside her prestigious private school. Seventeen years old and deeply loved. The same school my sister left when the bullying became unbearable.

The girl *is* my sister, who begs to stay home.

'I hated it too, bub, just like you,' I say, 'but you have to go.'

She has thick, ropey scars on her forearm. Just like me.

Mum hangs up. Minutes pass. I'm still sitting on the floor locking and unlocking my phone screen. I'd stopped myself from watching the videos all night. I knew I shouldn't, they'd make me sick. But the images played over and over in my mind anyway.

Little boys tied up and tear-gassed.

The sickening crack.

'Please, I can't breathe.'

What's the point of protecting my headspace now? Death and violence in all their forms press in close to my body. So do the walls of my room. Pulling the blankets off my bed to cover me, the woman says, close your eyes. You have uni tomorrow. I ignore her. Just once, then I'll be able to sleep.

Earlier that day

I slump into the lecture theatre late. Make sure not to sit next to anyone who'll talk to me. The woman is calling me but I ignore her.

Thank fuck, the lecturer is Aboriginal. She starts with the 'this is me, this is my mob' introduction. And I release the unease from my shoulders.

'I might not look how you expect an Aboriginal person to look but that doesn't make me any less blak,' she says.

I side-glance at the other students – no visible reactions. I chastise myself for always assuming the worst.

She plays a video of Alison Whittaker reciting her poem 'A Love Like Dorothea's'. Her words beautiful, true, subversive. Over beautiful sweeping shots of rivers, coasts and desert. I lean forward on the cool, hard desk. A panning shot of a coastal road. Then comes those images. Videos I promised myself I'd never watch again. A little boy being pushed to the ground by three big corrections officers. Cutting before the part where they forcibly strip him naked. Followed by a boy with a hood over his head. Tied by wrists, ankles, neck to a chair that looks like a medieval torture device.

The woman's face pops up on my iPad just when I need her. Muddy eyes lock in my gaze. Look at me, she says, it'll be over soon. Don't look at it. Chew on your tears before they make it to your face.

Last week

I wasn't much better. In a tutorial room where two of the walls are made of windows. One, to my left, looks out over trees and a carpark. The other, to my right, looks back into the hallway. I'm the oldest person in this room by a long way. Everyone else is under twenty. Apart from our tutor, who I've decided I like because she doesn't shave her legs. On the first week she stood at the front of the room and told us, 'There are no wrong answers. C'mon, don't be afraid to say what comes to your mind. Everyone's opinion is equally valid here.'

Now in that spot is a giant, roll-down screen projecting for us the film clip for 'Treaty' by Yothu Yindi. Familiarity washes over me. Yidaki sounding out over '90s rock-'n'-roll was the sound of a thousand barbecues, car trips, community events and even weddings. Like the sound of Ray Warren calling a Broncos game. Or my aunts discussing who from back home was 'jumping the back fence'. 'Treaty, yeah! Treaty, now!' was a refrain that had wrapped me up and rocked me to sleep in my infancy.

'Please discuss at your tables,' our tutor says.

In the room the blinds roll up automatically and I can see the woman at the window, looking at me.

'I've never heard that song before,' says the kid sitting beside me. That's how I think of everyone at my table: kids. Sometimes they seem so young, fresh-faced, unsure, that I feel an overwhelming affection. Other times I want to put them in time-out. 'It must be something indie,' he said, doubling down.

Laugh with shock, disbelief and a hint of cruelty. 'It's an Australian classic, actually.' The woman narrows her eyes at me. Today they're green and washed out by the sun. How are they to know? she reminds me. They don't know what you know, they don't live in your world. They're just kids.

Back then

the girl was me. At eleven years old I'm sitting in another classroom with another teacher at the front. One who absolutely shaves her legs, although we never see them under her severe black slacks. The type of woman who tells me, 'That's not very nice,' when I explain to the class that my family calls January 26 Invasion Day.

It's a hot and sticky summer. The rows of louvres are wide open. Time for my least favourite part of the social-studies yearly cycle. Indigenous Australia. Having yourself explained at you by dowdy, unkind teachers is a disconcerting experience. You, a living, breathing human, become an anthropologised other. You're told who and what you are by the education system of a colonial government that's still perpetuating a slow-motion genocide against you. And they expect you to listen politely and take notes. Don't forget to include a margin and the date.

The heading on the glossy textbook in front of me reads something like 'Effects of Colonisation on Indigenous Australians'. So, I'm hopeful that this year my mouth won't feel like it's filling up with invisible peanut butter to stop me from speaking. I know all about this topic. Having just returned from spending some of my summer school holidays in Mitchell, on Country.

On Country: Indigenous peoples don't view the land like Europeans do. They believe they can't own land because they are part of the land.

The textbooks don't tell you about the bodily feeling when you're on Country for the first time in a year. They don't know that there's an invisible line between Roma and Mitchell, and that once I cross it every cell in my body starts to sing. That when my feet hit the ground, electric energy rockets up my legs. I always twitch in my sleep for the first few nights. What the textbooks don't tell you is that all humans are fed by, animated by, non-localised consciousness. It's the same consciousness that's in the trees, mountains, rivers, dirt. White historians can't see that every single thing in the world is connected. They don't know that for every single one of us our 'soul' exists outside of our bodies. It's in the people around us. It's in the landscape. I just happen to know where mine is.

Mum's read *Blood on the Wattle* before the drive from Brisbane to Mitchell. So, she's in fine form as our Toyota Pajero speeds past fields of milo, cabbage, bundled-up cotton. She knew all about the massacres anyway, she reckons. From our old people. And from the archaeological reports she gets as part of her job. Rock paintings, artefacts, mass graves. They're all out there, buried knowledge, held by Country.

'If you turn left at that road and keep going south, there was a massacre,' she tells Aunty. My brother and I peer fearfully down that road as we pass it. As if colonial stockmen might start chasing the car with whips and shotguns.

'There was a battle at the base of that hill. All around here blackfullas fought and died.'

'Can't we play I spy?' my brother asks.

'No, look here, they massacred your ancestors around here,' she said as we pass through Yuleba.

Mum made sure I knew my history and I was glad my classmates would be hearing it too. We're taking turns to read paragraphs of the textbook out loud to the class. Everyone speaks at a gratingly slow pace so I read ahead to my part.

A large percentage of the aboriginal population died after the First Fleet arrived. Only a very small percentage of this was due to the frontier wars. Aborigines were not used to sugar and alcohol. Far more of the aborigines died due to diseases, such as smallpox, than they did in skirmishes with the settlers. Their bodies were incapable of fighting off the diseases European people brought with them.

Lies. Flat-out, blatant, glossy lies.

'Nadia, read now please.' The teacher's voice is far away.

Tongue flat against the bottom of mouth, thick and heavy. Can't say a word back. Not inside my body anymore. Everything around has turned unreal like I'm looking through a window at heatwaves on the highway. Everyone's watching. Can't make eye contact. Stare down at the calculator screen.

That's when I see the woman for the first time.

You live in two worlds, she says. One with the hidden truth. One with the constructed truth.

Now

the woman washes the beige from her fingers and picks up a bright pink sponge. Working quickly, I pat, pat, pat the bottom of the egg shape across my face. Spreading my make-up, modern-day ochre, warpaint, across my skin before it dries into an unworkable mess. I meet the eyes of my reflection one last time before I leave for uni. This is a different time. Things have changed, I remind myself. The narrative has moved on and people are much better educated. It's a hard subject for you at the best of times. You're too sensitive. Remember, be kind to others.

Minutes later

I slide into another uncomfortable chair in another stark, institutional room. There are no windows, so harsh fluorescent lights buzz overhead. The desk is too low for me. I have to slump and hunch to write my notes. Discussion begins. I breathe out, preparing to be discussed by the kids who learned from the coloniser's textbook. I'm glad to be sitting next to a familiar face.

Equal and welcomed opinions fly.

On literary prizes one says, 'They haven't been doing this very long, so the longer they do it, the more recognition they'll get.' They've only been storytelling and creating art for over a hundred thousand years. But sure, a few more years then we'll be experienced enough to be prize-worthy, I don't say.

Can't be kind, disengage.

'You know, I'm feeling really triggered by the lecture yesterday,' familiar face says to me. Relief. They do get it.

I say, 'I was too. It's really hard for me to see footage of the Don Dale torture at the best of times. Let alone without warning. Why were you triggered?'

'I just think,' she's riled up, speaking angrily, 'the lecturer should've acknowledged both sides of her heritage. She's obviously white. She looks white. Why would she stand up there saying "I'm black"? She didn't have to be so angry about it either.'

I look for the woman. All I find in the black mirrors of my devices are my own watery, exhausted eyes.

RED PLASTIC CHAIRS

AMY DUONG

The plastic chair is a Vietnamese cultural institution. If you've never seen one, then I am not sure if my description will do it justice. It has a square top with a hole straight through the middle and four legs of the cheapest plastic you've ever seen. It comes in a range of colours, but the best ones are always red.

Some of the chairs are short and replicate squatting height (good for washing vegetables over your garden bed). Others are tall (normal chair height) and require you to hunch forward so you don't overbalance. The Vietnamese plastic chair is cheap and versatile, and it goes with absolutely no-one's decor. It weighs almost nothing; it represents so much. It is an ambassador of Vietnamese street food, a loyal companion to all good phở. It is culture. It is nostalgia. Sometimes, it is even a makeshift bin.

For Vietnamese families in Australia, the chair is an integral part of community life. Lending a stack of chairs establishes a social contract that says: 'Let's begin a back-and-forth of favours until one of us dies.' The survivor will then bring a stack of chairs to the funeral as a final gesture of goodwill, and just in case all of Springvale decides to show up.

I don't own any plastic chairs myself and would have no idea where to buy them. For me, they serve a personal rather than functional purpose. They are cues, keys to memories I thought I had forgotten. One glimpse of that deep red (Is it for luck? Prosperity? Longevity?) and suddenly I am on the streets of Sài Gòn, petrol fumes swirling around me. One glance and I am eight years old, huddled over a Game Boy while my uncle sings 'Careless Whisper' on his home karaoke machine. I see tea ceremonies, funerals, family barbecues; the plastic is in my DNA. No doubt one day these chairs will fill the oceans, but for now they float through my memories, weighing almost nothing but carrying so much.

—

In the spring of 2011, my mother called to tell me my aunty had died.

'Oh,' I said before pausing a very long time. 'Are you okay?'

I had at that moment approximately ninety Vietnamese words and none of them were condolences.

'Okay,' she said before pausing just as long. 'Did you go to uni today?'

I said I had but I was lying. 'Good,' she said. 'Can you bring some chairs when you come down?'

'The red ones?' I asked.

'Yes, the red ones.'

'Okay,' I said, 'I'll come at five o'clock.'

'Okay, good,' she said and there was another long pause. I reached for my ninety words again.

'I'm sorry that she died.'

'It's okay,' my mother said. Then, before I could say anything else, she was gone.

—

My aunty was the oldest of my mother's siblings, and when she died she had already survived so much. As a teenager, she had fled from China to Vietnam, where she watched her country fall to the communists. In 1987 she and my mother's family clambered onto a fishing boat in the middle of the night to set sail for an uncertain future. A few years later she ended up in Melbourne's south-east. It was there that I knew her.

I am exaggerating slightly when I say that I knew her. I didn't know her well. I knew that she went to church on Sundays and that she spoke Vietnamese with a Chinese accent. I knew that she didn't smile in photos and that she kept her pension hidden in Danish biscuit tins because she didn't trust the banks. I knew that she wore dentures and that she watched the Australian Open. I am fairly sure that she believed in ghosts.

After she died, I watched my mother clean out her room. Her drawers were lined with clothes that had never been worn, all the tags still attached. The clothes themselves were not remarkable. Just a few polyester coats preserved for the sake of preservation.

My mother put them in a pile to donate to charity. Then, on a red plastic chair, she started another pile. These were the clothes that had been worn. This pile was small and it was made of shabby jumpers and homemade shirts. I could see where holes had been patched again and again. I ran my fingers over the sleeves; I touched the fraying seams. They felt so fragile. I tried to picture my aunty wearing them but it was almost unbearable. I made an excuse and left the room.

Standing in the hallway, I thought about the red pocket I had been given that year and how I had squandered it on such frivolous things. I thought about the speeding fines, bubble tea runs, *Transformers* at the IMAX. I felt guilty and childish. I forced myself to go back and look at her things one more time. The afternoon sun shone through the window. The plastic chair was like a plinth, exposing the contents of a life barely lived.

—

When I was eight my cousin told me that my aunty had walked from China to Vietnam and met a witch who put a curse on our family. 'That's why she doesn't have children,' he said, looking up from his Tamagotchi. I thought it sounded exciting, like something out of *Deltora Quest*. I asked her about it one afternoon.

'Tua Ee, is it true?'

She was sitting on a red plastic chair, the short kind, and she was tying bean curd into knots. She thrust a bowl into my hands. 'Either help or go away.'

I dropped the bowl and ran. I never asked again.

The morbid curiosity I had felt was short-lived. Deep down I knew that her life was unknowable to me, just as my grandparents' and parents' lives would always be. They never talked about history except in the odd mention of vague horrors: pirates, camps, the Tết Offensive. But these were only spectres and they lingered for merely moments before disappearing completely.

My life was not like theirs and could never be. I was born in Australia and all that I had ever known existed within its lucky boundaries. Their lives were split across continents, with pieces held captive somewhere distant and unreachable. Our generational gap was real and it grew wider with each passing year. They did not want to bridge that gulf by sharing their stories. The past did not embolden them to.

As I grew older, I also realised that I was not blameless. I had contributed to the growing divide. The languages my family spoke were languages I was shedding, deliberately at first but then completely by accident. I was like other immigrant children I knew who had been raised on *Cheez TV* and starved of representation. Australian perfection looked like *Dolly* magazine and *Home and Away*; it sounded like Kylie and Savage Garden. I wanted to speak that language too. I wanted to answer my mother's calls on the bus without drawing attention. Being multilingual did not make me feel accomplished, and when my parents sent me to Vietnamese school on Sunday mornings I slept at the back of the class and resented them. On days I felt brave, I skipped class entirely and walked to the milk bar to spend my red pockets on Wizz Fizz. When my elders spoke to me in Teochew and Vietnamese, I responded in English. This happened more and more, until one day – as if someone had taken them while I wasn't looking – I realised that almost all my native words were gone.

—

Thank you. Happy new year. Roast pork. Sugar-cane juice. These are some of the words I still know. *Oh my god. Studying business. Not yet married.* Those I had to learn for special occasions.

Some of the phrases I knew were so ingrained that I spoke them reflexively.

'Hello Tua Ee,' I would say when I saw my aunty (always by title, never by name).

'Have you eaten?' she would ask. I would put my hand on my stomach and nod. 'I have eaten.'

Occasionally she would try to ask me something more specific. 'What are you going to do when you graduate?' I would pause for a long time before shaking my head in defeat. I knew that I was too late. The ties that bind had come undone.

—

When my mother called to say that my Tua Ee had died I knew that my life would be no different. I put my phone in my pocket, climbed out of bed and went looking for the great stack of chairs. I had to move dozens of boxes to get to them because my parents are hoarders. I found a brand-new Tiger rice cooker, New Year's Eve paraphernalia from 2004 and multiple VCRs. The chairs were in a corner, covered by a huge bin liner. I unveiled them like they were a priceless statue at an auction.

That night, I drove to Tua Ee's house with the chairs in the boot of my car. My cousins had already arrived and were smoking by the side of the house. They were adults but they hid their habits from their mothers, partly out of guilt and partly out of fear. Dozens of cars lined the street and people hurried back and forth carrying pots of food. There were kids running in the yard and I even heard my uncle laugh. Out of respect, no-one tiptoed around the dead.

I saw people I hadn't seen before and wondered where they had come from. I saw a man walk up the driveway with a stack of plastic chairs in his arms. Beside him, a woman carried rolls of thin white gauze. I recognised that these were rituals, but I didn't understand them. At that moment, my mother stuck her head out a window and called my name. 'Bring the chairs in,' she said, 'more people are coming.'

'Okay, I'll do it in a bit.'

I wanted to stall the grief and the chaos so I lingered outside. I went over and joined my cousins in our ritual of keeping watch between puffs of smoke. Then my mother called my name again and I heard her outside slippers approaching. We scrambled to hide what we were doing, but it was not enough. Through the lingering smoke I saw my mother shake her head from side to side. I was sure that she was going to yell. I was even surer that we deserved it.

She opened her mouth and we braced ourselves. But then she closed it again without saying a word. Instead, she pulled up a red plastic chair and placed on top of it a bowl of carefully sliced fruit.

'We saved the sweetest fruit for you,' she said.

I sheepishly reached for the ninety words I knew. 'Thank you.'

'It's nothing,' she said.

But it was not nothing. I looked down at the bowl, with her silence still ringing in my ears. The red chair framed it in perfect symmetry. It looked like a painting in a gallery. All of a sudden I wanted to cry. Each piece of fruit had been cut so carefully that I could picture her with a Kiwi knife in her hands, jade bracelet knocking against her watch.

Maybe it was the selflessness of her silence. Or maybe it was because I had seen her sacrifices a million times before and never recognised them for what they were. But they were the language we still had in common, one that I understood. Her gentle gestures spoke so lovingly, I only wished that I deserved them. So I picked up the chair in my hands and brought it closer. It was so light. It weighed almost nothing. In that moment I saw it for what it was: an anchor to a place I knew I would not inhabit forever.

THE WISE MEN ON THE WIRELESS

NAKUL LEGHA

As a fresh-faced arrival to Australia aged nine, I tried everything to fit in. But in the process I turned myself into a middle-aged white man, thanks to an unhealthy and unsupervised childhood obsession with conservative talkback radio.

Lacking any real connection to my new home, I plunged myself into this curious, sun-kissed culture by suckling from the all-knowing teats of conservative talkback kings Stan 'the Man' Zemanek, John 'Golden Tonsils' Laws and Alan 'Parrot' Jones.

Like Homer's Sirens luring unwitting sailors, these men first entranced me from the tinny speakers in the back seat of Kuljit Uncle's '92 Corolla, the grand chariot in which my parents and I made our entrance into Australian life. It was a hot and muggy day. The backs of my thighs stung from the Corolla's hot pleather.

I was pinned under a heavy box of haldi-stained stainless-steel pots and Miss Mary, our beloved five-litre pressure cooker. But my mind was completely captivated by the powerful purr of the wise men on the wireless.

These were confident, articulate men who knew everything there was to know about being Australian. About being an Aussie battler. An Aussie father. An Aussie patriot. They spoke English and somehow managed to do it without a thick Indian accent. Most impressively, they were always right. Everyone who called in agreed with them. And if they didn't, they would be shouted at until they did. I wanted to wield that sort of power over my new classmates and teacher each time they put on mocking Apu accents and wobbled their heads when speaking to me.

I had no siblings, no friends or babysitters, and my parents were caught up in a losing game of musical chairs hunting down poorly paid shift work. So I found solace with Jonesy before school, Stan in the evenings, and Lawsie as a treat on holidays when school didn't clash with his mid-morning shift. What kind of idiot programmed Golden Tonsils during school hours anyway?

For the few who didn't spend their childhoods listening to talkback radio, these men were demagogues speaking to and from the heart of middle Australia. Like all battlers, they earned millions speaking up for the working class, had a direct line to those in power and brought in rivers of gold in advertising revenue for their stations.

The formula was a rich diet of creative insults and outrage over the ills of multiculturalism, Indigenous Australians, gay rights, welfare recipients and the general state of Australia. Throw in some

Slim Dusty bush ballads, and regular male callers who pretended to be women because it was a very novel and funny concept, and you had a perfect microcosm of modern Australia ripe to be plucked and studied by a chubby Indian boy with a bowl cut.

My lasting obsession was with Stan. I spent weeknights after school unwinding with Stan, curled up on the balcony of our tiny apartment, where the reception was better, holding the portable radio in one hand and a cold glass of Milo in the other.

Stan's grudges soon became my grudges. I followed the radio ratings closely (number one in three metro markets again, yes!). I was shocked when Jonesy defected to a rival station and would go head to head with our beloved station. I relished Stan's rivalry with fellow broadcaster Mike Carlton, who was, in Stan's eloquent words, 'a turd'. Like every kid, I picked sides and chose favourites. Ford vs Holden. Warney vs Murali. 2UE vs 2GB. Stan vs Mike. Lawsie vs Jones.

When people asked my nationality, I was sure to proclaim that I was 'Australian–Indian'. Stan was obsessed with testing the national allegiance of his ethnic callers and made a point of telling the Abduls, Tans or Kims who called in that the Australian always came before the hyphen. I shook my head in dismay when Mohammed from Campsie called in one night and said he was Lebanese–Australian. 'That's not how you speak to Stan,' I whispered to myself, swirling my Milo.

I bought a comically large Australian flag to hang proudly in my bedroom next to the much smaller Indian flag. I became that guy wearing the Aussie flag as a cape at every sports event and public gathering, desperate to show off my dinky-di bona fides.

When my parents started having doubts about the Australian experiment – something about no money, no jobs, no prospects – I agreed to move back to India on one condition: that they buy me every single one of the more than a hundred albums released by Slim Dusty over his career. We didn't move back. I can only assume the deciding factor was the prospect of further financial ruin at the hands of Australia's most beloved and industrious country-music artist.

Some kids dreamed of playing cricket for Australia while I fantasised about being a featured caller on Stan's show. Instead of doing homework, I spent hours hogging the home phone, stuck on hold trying to get through to Stan. I had my intro sorted: 'Hi Stan, yes, it's Nakul from Parramatta. I'm Australian–Indian and I love your show. That's right, I'm only ten years old! Your youngest listener? Haha, you bet. You know, I was thinking about what you said on dole bludgers getting disability pensions and ...'

I'm not sure what I was really thinking about dole bludgers on disability. I'm not sure I was even the intended audience for diatribes about welfare cheats, capital punishment or the way things were. But it didn't matter. I just wanted so badly to be, to feel and to be seen as Australian. And these were the first voices to tell me definitively how I could do that.

It turned out Stan didn't much like immigrants. Not many of my talkback heroes did. In fact, Stan was an advocate for a total ban on immigration while any Australian remained unemployed. In his ideal world, my parents and our pressure cooker would have been turned back by border control.

Would he have liked me if I'd got through to the show? Would he have approved of me?

I think so. I was different from the others. I made an effort. I did everything right. I was a patriot and I demanded patriotic perfection from those around me. Though I was fluent, I increasingly avoided speaking Hindi in public. I stopped going to the temple. I was embarrassed when Mum wore a salwaar kameez to Parra Westfield, and I sure as hell let her know. I impatiently corrected Dad's pronunciation when he offered to make Wedgie Mite on toast for breakfast or take us to Pijja Hut for dinner. I made sure that the red, white and blue of the Union Jack was always visible in front of the saffron, green and white of the Indian flag.

I never had Anglo friends over to our place, sparing them the stink of masala, the burden of eating our food with their delicate porcelain hands and making stilted small talk with my parents. I distanced myself from my Indian friends because they were so painfully rooted in the past, to the old culture, to those outdated traditions.

Instead, I filled up the empty vessel of my new cultural identity from a high-pressure hose of scummy nationalism. Once that vessel was full to the brim, I stuck the open end of the hose down my throat and gulped down Australia until I belched and bloated and pissed myself.

Red, white and blue.

THE CRYING SONG

KARLA HART

Names of deceased people are in this story, for my family.

I can't remember the first time I heard it. It was part of the fabric of my life. When we were little we just knew what to do – be quiet, use hand and eye gestures to communicate and be respectful as people were crying. We would sit and look at each other, as we knew the grief was from losing someone who meant something so much that the deep crying, like a song, would go on for days and weeks.

I lived with my grandmother, mostly in a house on Richardson Street, Gnowangerup, in the Great Southern of Western Australia. I would go over the fence, into the laneway and through a hole in another fence to see my mum and my sisters. Up the road from my house lived my Aunty Joyce and Uncle Aden and my older first bloods, who were more like siblings. Next door to them were my Uncle Billy and Aunty Annette, a couple of doors down from them my Uncle Eugene and Aunty Martha, and through the laneway again was my Pop Bill and his wife, Aunty Liza. In the actual town lived my nan's other son and so many other aunties and uncles and cousins.

With Mum and her family being used to living all together in Gnowangerup, Jerramungup, Ongerup, and on the missions and reserves, we spent a lot of time still living together even though we had our own houses. We had many nights – up to weeks, even – at my Aunty Joyce's, sometimes with her brother and often with her son and niece, and then we'd all go back to our houses. I remember times when kids were acting up or struggling, our mob thought nothing of letting them stay for months on end, sometimes years, with other family and even in other towns – with uncles and aunties they had a good connection with. Because we were one big family. We loved each other dearly, everyone helped each other with food, money and transport.

Sometimes when my nyitiyung (non-Indigenous) friends or colleagues comment on another funeral I have to attend, saying 'You've had a bad year', it's like, no not really: our cousins are brothers and sisters; aunts and uncles are like mums and dads, and pops and nans are all of ours. How do you distinguish love for your immediate family when, in our kinship way, everyone is considered immediate family?

Now back to ngoony-ngoony (crying).

Back when family always came to tell you of a close passing in person (way before people posted the bad news on Facebook to the hour, let alone the day, which upsets so many of our mob today), you could hear the crying before they even got to the door. It was like a cloud travelling, a bubble of grief; when you heard it, you knew it was someone close. They would cry for the pain, the loss, and then cry bringing the news to you for your pain, then this would continue as each person came through that door. So it never really ended. Just when you thought the crying was finished, someone else might rock up from a long way and everyone would cry again together, crying for each person and their connection to the passed loved one. Or someone might start up whimpering on their own, softly, then others would join. It would build and become rhythmic, like a song, with ebbs and flows and crescendos, an opera of grief between us all.

It's hard to truly describe the sound of the wailing or ngoony-ngoony. It's a crying song that comes in stages. Tragic news causes song that is sharp and pure pain, a harrowing cry mixed with howling and screaming; then the song is consistent in its overwhelming grief and sadness. A beautiful yet haunting sound of someone so devastated – almost like a love letter in the form of a cry to whoever had passed.

For dead boy or dead girl, as Mum used to say because she didn't say their names, this crying would go on for two weeks on and off, as generally our mob doesn't have the funeral for two weeks. It gives people time to grieve together before the funeral, to travel, to organise and to come to terms with burying this loved one. Time to go sit with them, to say last goodbyes, to kiss them, to tell them things and to cry on them before they are committed back to boodja (country).

It is a two-week ceremony, and during those weeks family would open their homes up for those that travelled, mattresses would be put on floors and we would spend time eating together – often kangaroo meat and damper, making everything stretch. As well as the crying, we would play with cousins we don't get to see much, the old people would reminisce and share their memories, funeral decisions would be made (but never on the first couple of days): what day, which plot, who would carry the body and which Noongar pastor would conduct the service. Reconnections would be made, people who had gone to live away from country remembering who they were and how strong their bloodlines were, and lots of laughing and lovely memories would be made in between the crying.

The practices of a two-week grieving period are very old, and by the time I was born my grandparents had adapted to being on country to being on missions, reserves, and then in town. Death, for thousands of years, has been a ceremony for our people and continues to be, and, as our elders have, we continue to adapt.

I stayed home on country until I finished Year 12 and left for the big city, Perth, and went straight into a corporate world. Many times, when I applied for funeral leave, I was made to feel as if I was milking the system and that I didn't really need to go. Going home for the death, staying a few days, coming back to work in the city, and then going back for the funeral and staying a few more days.

Nyitiyung way, you're expected to just go for the funeral from work. Sometimes when I left Perth and stayed home till funeral day I nearly lost my job, or I used all my leave for the year. I had to go to many funerals, and many times had to make ends meet on leave without pay. And that was only the financial burden of trying to survive, keep my rental and live in a white man's world.

The emotional effects were far worse.

There have been times when I couldn't go home for the two weeks but could go only for the funeral. If this happens, you cry on your own. It is hard to explain how much you miss your family's arms holding you in this lonely time, right down to the little kids who would come sit on your lap or hug you, as I did to my elders once upon a time to try to ease their pain. You cry in a house and you feel suffocated by walls. I have wailed alone and sometimes wailed so loudly and for so long that I wondered if the neighbours might call the police. I have made myself sick wailing alone.

When you are with family they let you go crying, but if it gets so intense it's dangerous, they will step in, they will stop you from being sick. When you go home, grief is monitored by family and balanced with the joy of being in one and everybody looking after each other. You exhaust yourself, and by the time the funeral comes you are okay, then the funeral itself brings back the wailing, like from the first day, but that is from the body finally going into the boodja. Then we cover the grave up and pat down the sand and place the flowers. We meet again the next day to take them off, and we do it properly and slowly, without people waiting at a wake. You sweep around the grave with a bush broom and the soft crying song is present in its last notes before everyone goes home; it is almost like a warm-down, and it eventually stops as you perform physical tasks that settle you to travel safe.

After the funeral you have come full circle with grief, you have shared memories and laughter, you have been strangely refreshed, and you have honoured that loved one and respected your grief with time. You go back to work and feel sad but okay to get up and keep going.

When I haven't been able to go through those two weeks first, I go back to work after the funeral and I am still walking around carrying grief, I haven't been able to process it; if one person says 'Are you okay?' I cry. I have sick days and I never really feel right, and I feel like I missed an important time with my family and I grieve for that too. And the older I get, the more I understand that our bodies and our spirits need this to stay strong; it is old wisdom that has continued to be practised for a reason. It almost exhausts grief out of our system and weaves love through so that it doesn't wound us for life.

I could say so much more about wailing, about sorry business, but I'll leave with it being a constant Western-world conflict for us Noongars. Even though I say two weeks, some family end up staying for months after the funeral and enrolling their kids in school in town. We continue to go to the cemetery together to do up the graves, especially on the anniversary of death, mother's and father's days, birthdays and before Christmas, to remember our loved ones and to provide other times to cry together to keep healing and to stay strong. So it doesn't spill over too much, we keep our mental health in check and depression at bay, especially with sudden deaths, murders and suicides and living away from country.

I have noticed funerals getting quieter from when I was younger (for many reasons, including succumbing to Western-world etiquette), but there are still wailers. I am a wailer – I feel it deep within my soul, it erupts from me, I am my grandmother's child, I cry naturally for my people, I even wail at times when I hear of a death in custody or a young person I don't know. I just feel it.

This sorry business part of our culture can be used by anyone to help heal hearts and spirits, as universally people need each other and grief shouldn't be rushed.

Wailing is a song to the spirits to send them off on their journeys to the next world, so they know how important they are to us and so the spirits that await them know they are coming and they are our people. It is a vibration cry that reverberates from one world to the next, connecting both worlds for a moment in time.

THE WORLD SMELLS LIKE FISH GUTS

JASON PHU

One time there were more fish in the sea. Even before our sinkers hit the bottom, a few trevally or yellowtail would be on our hooks. Now there are no fish, and all we have is each other.

I've gone fishing with my dad at Palm Beach since I was born. I know they don't want us there, but I take my dad's lead and fish until my hands bleed. We eat rubbery Vietnamese spam with shallots and chillies and soy sauce in bread rolls in the park afterwards. Carefree barbecuers in their swimmers toss an inflatable ball around; we're a curious sight for them, still dressed in our five am hoodies and covered in fish guts. They will never know the taste of shame and defiance that a piece of rubbery grey mystery meat can conjure. At the time, I think this feeling is what it means to be an adult, but for my father's generation it is something to be swallowed like a bitter herbal pill.

My mum came with us once but never again, because 'this is boring as hell'. My uncle – her brother – came with us another time but didn't last a hundred metres out the dock before feeling seasick. They're northerners, from China, land people who don't fuss with bodies of water that aren't rivers or streams.

When we get home my dad cleans any fish we've caught. Slicing the belly open and easing the guts out. One time, my dog and I were watching him do this and a small, prawn-like bug crawled out of the fish's mouth, a common parasite that lives on fish tongues. My dad stopped what he was doing and we all watched it crawl along the concrete. My dog quickly scooped it up and ate it. There is no natural order to things, there is only what dogs will eat and what they won't eat.

After my dad's done with cleaning the fish, he always puts the fish guts on his chilli plant in our backyard, along with some eggshells, and then he pisses on it; he says it is good for the plant. My mum is watching from nearby, shaking her head. My father always repeats to me, 'Make sure you wash your hands after cutting chillies if you need to go pee.'

My dad was born in Vietnam, although his father's family was originally from the Hainan islands, on the southern tip of China. They were fishing people, the sea was their home. He told me stories of a fishing village that were so vivid I thought he was raised there. I went there a few years ago with my girlfriend. We were living in Chongqing at the time and decided to visit for a holiday after I told her some of my dad's stories. We ate grilled seafood from street barbecues and drank old sour coconuts every day. We lay on beaches, crammed like sardines with other holiday-makers. The water was like the warm stale coconut water we drank. When I told the locals I was from Australia, some of them sneeringly referred to it as the Bali of Russia. When I got back I told my dad how different it was to what it was like for him growing up; he said he'd never set foot in Hainan before.

My dad's constant joke to Mum before we go fishing is 'We'll stop at the fish market on the way home so there's something to eat.' He really does just enjoy sitting around in the tinnie with a line and watching the colour of the sky change, trying a new beer a cousin told him about ('This is a trendy new beer called Coopers'). It doesn't matter if any fish are caught – of course, that's what everyone says when there are no nibbles. Sometimes a pelican lands next to us and we chuck it a couple of fish that are too small to keep. Usually, it leaves unimpressed with our fishing skills.

The day before we go fishing Dad prepares the burley. The burley is a mixture you throw into the water to lure fish. He gets a big plastic bucket and puts chicken feed and fish oil in and mixes it by hand for an hour. It smells like an old wet dog that has taken a bath in a tub of sardines.

He then prepares the hooks and sinkers. He sits in the basement carefully picking out each sinker and hook; they are indistinguishable to me in their brown rust. There are a few shiny new ones, but we save those for maybe next time, a concept that is beyond my comprehension. I am peeking around the corner, too scared to disturb this delicate ritual. I am a little boy, so everything my father does is mysterious. He threads the lines in and out of the sinkers and the hooks; I cannot fathom how this magic works. Finally, he picks the different rods he will take, examining each one, top to bottom. Then, placing them carefully next to each other, grouping them into two sets of three, he binds them with ancient ropes of flaking rubber bands.

He never teaches me any of this. Or maybe it's because I never ask to be taught.

That is a lie. There is one time, when I'm much older, I ask him to show me. He seems annoyed and I'm aware this will be a one-time instruction. He shows me and I watch. Young bird watches older bird to learn how to catch fish. The knot is easy and I copy it without fault. The next time we go fishing I forget how to do it and I'm too ashamed to ask again.

There's a story of a young bird that watches an old bird catch little fish from a river. Young bird is hungry. Young bird wants to learn from old bird how to catch fish. Old bird teaches young bird. Young bird learns easily. Young bird catches a big fish the next day and swallows it whole. The fish is too heavy and young bird falls into the river, weighted by the fish. Young bird drowns, tiny fish and little crabs consume young bird. Old bird watches from a rock. Old bird never teaches another young bird how to catch fish.

Eventually I stopped fishing. The excitement of waking up at five am to drive two hours gave way to the familiar nauseating drone of hangovers that youth discover. People stop caring about things from the past when there are no more fish in the sea.

One thing I will never forget: To catch a big fish you don't just put a shitty little bit of bait on your hook. You get a big rod that makes a terrible whirring sound, like a gurgling water demon. You catch a small yellowtail with your smaller rod. And you hook two hooks into the spine of that small yellowtail. The yellowtail lets out a terrible wet scream, a scream you imagine any creature would make if it were impaled by a hook through its spine. It makes me sick. You cast out the fish on the big rod and you wait. You hear that terrible whirring sound and you reel it in. What you usually get back is one half of the fish you cast out. You imagine how big that lost fish is, how its scales shimmer from the depths, and how it struck the little yellowtail with its rows and rows of teeth. I am a little boy, so I imagine an ancient Chinese dragon.

The old homeless drunk at the jetty where we always docked once told me a story about a dragon that lived under the sea. The dragon felt sad that its children, the fish, were being caught by people, but it understood that the people needed to be fed. So it sacrificed itself and transformed into a thousand fish to be caught in their place. Many people heard of all the fish that had come from the dragon's body and went to the sea to catch the fish with rods and nets. They fished away the dragon's gift and kept on fishing the dragon's children until there were none left. And that is why there are no fish now. The old drunk isn't there anymore either, and my dad didn't like me talking to him anyway, he says 'drunks are bad people'.

The second thing I will never forget: My dad and his brother pull up a stingray, it fills the whole tinnie, with just enough room for us to stand. They're laughing to each other at the ridiculous situation, they're laughing like the two best friends they are, like schoolchildren at lunchtime. For a moment they are individuals free from their histories, although I have no understanding of this then. The sun is out but there is a cool breeze, a few wispy clouds rolling around without purpose. There are already enough fish in our icebox for a feast with our families tonight. I am six and I am scared of this alien in our tinnie, I am screaming at them to throw it back. I piss my pants. They laugh harder than before at the sight of me as they throw the stingray back in.

One more thing – well, actually two: I remember one of the last times I fished, sitting in the tinnie with my dad. There was a breeze gently bobbing our boat up and down. I had been out the night before so my stomach was a violent storm, my head was thunder and lightning, my mouth tasted like fish guts. The sun was harsh, caning us with its heat. We had caught nothing. My dad was smiling and sipping at his Crown Lager. He was smiling even when there weren't nibbles. There were no waves, but I leant over the side and threw up. 'Good burley,' my dad muttered to himself.

In my memories, we are eating fish and chips on the astroturf at the fish markets. It's where my mum first worked when she arrived in Australia and where my dad met her, but that's another story. My dad brings over half a dozen oysters and squeezes a lemon wedge over them. The seagulls swoop down and try to steal our chips and fly away while squirting jets of white liquid shit. I never saw Mum work at the fish markets; by the time I was born she was working at the chicken shop.

There's no parable for our lives, there is only fish guts and chicken salt.

LOVE IN THE TIME OF GRANDMOTHER

SITA WALKER

From the moment I was born, my grandmother made me feel as though the moon hung in the sky just so that she could find me in the dark. In November of 1981, my father drove my mother, with my grandmother by her side, to the town hospital for my birth. The last of four children, I was determined to make a speedy entry into the world, and as my mother rode the elevator up to the birthing ward, the midwife urged her not to push: 'Hold it in, Mrs Walker, hold it.' My grandmother leant over and famously muttered in Farsi, 'Don't listen to her. If the baby wants to come, let her come.' What the baby wants the baby gets.

My grandmother had five children. She raised them in a small flat in Pune, in the western Indian state of Maharashtra, after leaving Iran when her husband died of tuberculosis. My mother was two years old when they moved into the flat with my grandmother's older sister, who had five children of her own and was recently widowed herself. Two mothers, ten children, and a lot of plain rice was how my mother grew up. She and my grandmother emigrated to Australia by ship in 1966, crossing the Indian Ocean to a new world. Shortly after arriving in Sydney, my mother met my father, a Knox Grammar old boy and long-legged grandson of an Irish preacher. As they say, the rest is history.

Australia in the '60s was a far cry from the heaving, rickshaw-laden streets of India and, on their first date, Mum famously asked Dad if the Prime Minister had died. When he said, 'No, why do you ask?' she said, 'I thought the country was in mourning, there are no people on the street!' It turns out there were enough people staring at them as they walked hand in hand to make Mum feel like a museum curiosity.

Sydney soon became too busy for their liking. I grew up in Toowoomba. We lived in a large breezy Queenslander with four big bedrooms, a sleep-out, an office, and a formal lounge with 'good' furniture that we only sat on if guests came over. When Mum fell pregnant with me, nine years after her last baby, my eldest sister wailed, 'You're so old, Ma! What will my friends think?' Even her doctor chastised her. 'Mrs Walker, you know you're no spring chicken. You must know how this happens by now?' Mum was thirty-eight. Nowadays she'd just be getting started. With a full-time job and three older children to raise, Mum did the most sensible thing she could – asked my grandmother to move in and take care of the baby.

Indian grandmothers do not subscribe to Western theories of controlled crying, or set feeding times and bed times. What the baby wants the baby gets. I was rocked to sleep in my grandmother's arms and carried all day if I cried. I fed when I pleased and slept when I was tired. As a chubby toddler and then a knobbly kneed child, I was lawless. I could do whatever I liked, so long as my grandmother could see me doing it. The rest of the family was busy with school and work and friends and life, but she followed me everywhere and fed me by hand while I played. I never had to sit down to breakfast or lunch. I could eat it in the garden, or on the steps, or in my toy box, so long as I was eating.

We had a large yard, and my grandmother and I spent a lot of time in it. While I played on the purple carpet made by our jacaranda, she tended to the vegetables and herbs down the side of the house. Potatoes, parsley, tomatoes, chillies. Coriander, constantly going to seed. We had an enormous camphor laurel as well, and she would crush the leaves in her hand and thrust them under my nose so I could smell the camphor. I grew up shoeless, watching her hosing the garden while I made daisy chains and caught clover moths or slaters in jars. I built a cubbyhouse in the old tennis shed and spend entire days brewing grass tea and leaf stew. Naturally, Grans was the grateful recipient of my fine catering. At the top of the back stairs, she had a cheap birdcage that housed two budgerigars called Bert and Ernie. Every few weeks she would feel sorry for Bert and Ernie, stuck there in the cage, and she would let them fly free. The next week she would be missing them so much, she'd buy another Bert and Ernie to replace them.

My grandmother called for me relentlessly if I was out of sight, especially in her later years when she was less mobile. It wasn't unusual for a neighbour to drop in and say, 'Dolly! Sita is in our yard, love! Stop calling her!' That was her name, Dolly – Dowlat at birth. She would say, 'Okay, thank you, now come in and have some dahl and pakora.' Mama Doll is how she came to be called, by neighbours all up and down our street. 'You were off at school and Mama Doll had a fall in the garden,' we would hear some days, from Gail on the left, or Anne on the right. 'Ian was out on a call, fixing the powerlines, but he came home to pull her up. We've sorted her out, don't you worry,' they would tell Mum. Mama Doll was everyone's grandmother.

I never found her stifling. I never felt guilty that she was worrying about me, or compelled to answer straightaway. It was just how we did things. I did as I pleased, and she called me. In the mornings, she rolled and fried hot chapatis for me, with fresh butter and jam, and at night she brought me sliced apples to eat in bed while I read. She put her soft hands on my back or my forehead and said prayers over me in her warm voice. On her wooden bed in the sleep-out, she would lie back watching the cricket on her tiny, wall-mounted television. When the Aussies won she would discuss the score gleefully with my brother and cousins. She was proud of the soil that grew up her grandchildren.

My grandmother had a bucket of chocolate eclairs, fruit tingles and peppermints under her bed that she would dish out to whoever was sitting with her. If I ever wanted to go to the shops, she would pull out her grey leather purse from the side of her recliner and give me a wad of her pension money. Whatever she had I could have. She never tried to improve me or check my manners, nag me to practice the piano, finish my homework or clean my room. She just wanted to know exactly where I was at all times.

When I was a teenager and no longer in the bug-catching, grass-tea catering business, she would telephone the coffee shops in town, or even the cinema, to find me. There I'd be, trying to look sophisticated, sipping my cappuccino and chatting with some boy, when the barista would call out, 'Is there a Sita here? Your grandmother wants to know when you'll be home.' My friends thought she was hysterical. Needless to say, their nannas did not call the cinemas. To this day, twenty years after my grandmother's death, there are friends and family who call me Sita-Koo, which means 'Where is Sita?' like it is my actual name.

My grandmother had never been to school, but had taught herself to read and write English. My dad taught her that the earth moved around the sun, and she was amazed. She taught me to love everyone. When Princess Diana died, she went into weeks of mourning. I'm glad she wasn't around to see Charles wed Camilla – I don't want to tell you what she used to call her, but there's a sailor blushing somewhere just thinking about it.

Slowly, she became too old to chase me, and too frail to get up from her bed and come to my room to kiss me goodnight, so I began going to her. I would check her bedside toilet chair, empty it and disinfect it. I would cut her fingernails and toenails. I would shower her, dry her, and help her powder herself and get dressed. I would brush her hair, tuck her into bed, kiss her goodnight, and say prayers for her while I held her hand or lay next to her with my arm across her chest. The years of making her grass tea turned into years of making actual tea. When I was out at coffee shops or the movies, I would bring home a roll of fruit tingles for her bucket. What the grandmother wants the grandmother gets.

In the weeks after she died I would find myself drowsily winding through the house to the sleep-out, to tuck her in and say goodnight. I would make it halfway through the formal lounge before I realised the person who had loved me without wanting to change a single thing about me was gone. Sometimes I would give the good furniture a kick.

Time moves it all, doesn't it? I left home, got married and had my own babies to chase after and call, here in our leafy hamlet of Brissy. My mother, now in her late seventies but sprightly and sassy as ever, has risen to the role of Grandmother-elect with cellular accuracy. Life is swirling and leaping all around me; it has never been more hectic. But I still miss her every day. Sometimes when I see a magpie watching me intently, or when the swallows on the school oval fly around me in circles as I walk across the field to my staffroom, I wonder. Sometimes in the shower, or just as I fall asleep, I think I hear her voice. There's a camphor laurel on the other side of the creek near my place.

The Sufi poet Rumi writes: On the day I die, when I'm being carried toward the grave, don't weep. Don't say, He's gone! He's gone! Death has nothing to do with going away. The sun sets and the moon sets, but they're not gone.

Two years ago, I was having lunch with some girlfriends of mine from school. We were talking about our lives, husbands, jobs, parents – the things you talk about intimately with your oldest friends. We got on to kids and responsibilities, and I said, 'Sometimes I feel guilty about giving mine so many chores. Childhood should be free! I never did a thing growing up, other than read books and play in the yard.' They all looked at me as the conversation stopped. One of them said, 'Are you kidding? You didn't do nothing! You took care of your grandmother every day. We all watched you do it.'

Funny, I always thought it was the other way around.

THE WEIRDO'S WIN

TRENT WALLACE

'Diversity' is certainly not a celebrated attribute in school. It is a slick term adopted by corporate machines. But in the real world it means being fucking weird and it means being a target – especially, as I discovered, if you live in a regional area.

But if you survive the years of awkward, embarrassing and devastating experiences, you will be rewarded. Those experiences will lay the foundation for a staunch yet empathetic character. This will be what sets you apart from your peers in work, and you'll have the skills to navigate difficult positions in life. You'll develop a thick skin, and kindness will be at the core of your values. You'll seek to be a positive force in the world. You will also be incredibly tough and be perceived as a threat, which you should be. You know how to survive and that can be scary to generic audiences.

If you are at all uncomfortable with any of this, lean in and ask yourself how you have treated those perceived as 'diverse'.

———

I grew up on the Central Coast of New South Wales; that's ninety kilometres from Sydney in distance, but about fifteen years in levels of acceptance. I was the fat, blak, left-handed, queer enigma that kids loved to taunt. Primary school was a nightmare. The playground held no playing for me, but represented hell – it was the platform for normality. I'd weave through games of handball, trying not to get hit by balls that were aimed at me, a seven-year-old kid. All because I was different.

I got through each day by thinking about home time. Our house was small, but it was my safe space.

My unconventional childhood was a house filled with music – from Mi-Sex's 'Computer Games' to anything by AC/DC. We didn't have any board games. No white picket fences. No glamorous holidays. My dad, who didn't own a suit and was covered in tattoos he'd collected in his teens, was studying at university and working part-time. He would sit at our dining table to do assignments and my mum would type up his work – she would use this as an opportunity to extend her learning informally. Mum kept the house together and once ended up hospitalised because she was going without food to ensure the rest of my family had enough to eat. I noticed she would avoid dinnertime with us, often busying herself with housework, sustained by a diet of cigarettes, sugary soft drink and, if the family budget permitted, Cadbury's peppermint chocolate. I'd later learn that the family budget was balanced on approximately $13,000 a year. An interesting command of the English language included sentences peppered with swear words. We didn't do your traditional things like having picnics or guests over.

Dad, an Aboriginal man, doesn't trust or enjoy many people. He speaks in strong, short sentences. Mum is more of a bubbly social butterfly, the person you call to dump your troubles on: a foul-mouthed goddess with a heart of gold.

I'd also be a regular visitor at my nana and pop's place, ten or so minutes away from my house. My nana would spend time with me, teaching me about the world and life. One time I asked her, 'Nana, are you rich?' to which she replied, 'What do you mean by rich, dear heart? Do you mean in possessions and money or in love and happiness?' This profound revelation still strikes me today. I felt rich in love from my family – they were what I sought solace in.

———

The morning school bus used to cause me a particular anxiety. I'd view it as transportation to torture. Looking back, it wasn't far short of a hearse driving me to my funeral, with my hopes all dead – dramatic much? But seriously, that's what it felt like. Except the bus wasn't slick or black, it was loud and annoying. One summer morning, when I got on it and tried to find a place to sit, grinning kids greeted me, motioning towards a seat. I looked up and smiled and thanked them – my bag was heavy with books and I didn't feel like standing. I recall feeling so shocked but grateful. Maybe I was finally making some friends. I trusted these kids, as they were older and weren't in any of my classes. So many thoughts as I waddled down the middle section of the bus. It was already a hot and sticky day, and as I went to sit I noticed a smell and looked down. The seat and surrounding floor had been smeared with dog shit. I had trod in some already. My polished brown Clarks shoes were a part of the school uniform and Mum had got them at Payless a few weeks earlier – they were a far cry from the Christian Louboutin shoes that adorn my feet today, but that's a different story. The bus was almost full and everyone was laughing at me. I found another seat, but the kid told me to go away and tried to push and kick me off it. He told me that I was disgusting. My face was red-hot and that added to the humour of the kids. For them, it was a prank to pass their morning. For me, it was a soul-destroying moment. My ears were burning and I wanted to cry, but I held it all in and felt like I was going to pass out. I ignored them all and focused on getting to school without crying.

Getting off the school bus, I hid behind a wall, only to be found by a parent I knew. Her kids were nice to me, but they didn't want to be my friends. They were dark-skinned and consequently bullied too – they didn't want me around bringing even more attention to them. Their mum comforted me and took me to a teacher. I begged them all: 'Please just let me go home, call my parents.' By now I was crying so hard that my nose was running as much as my eyes. The shame and embarrassment stung like nothing else had before. I had been humiliated in front of a whole school bus. A teacher escorted me to the library as I couldn't face a classroom. Distraught, with tear-stained cheeks and my stomach in knots, I was convinced everyone around me must've known what had occurred. The librarian, a rather unkind woman, told me I'd eventually have to go back to class. I just wanted to be home. By early afternoon, the librarian and teacher instructed me to go back to the classroom. Feelings of confusion and dismay rattled in my brain. Why hadn't my parents come to collect me? I later found out that the school, in a painful breach of its duty of care, had failed to notify my parents. Later, the mother who had found me called my mother to check in on me, believing that I was at home with my parents.

As I sat uncomfortably in the back of the classroom, I heard a familiar thunder get closer to my classroom. A Harley-Davidson. My dad emerged in the doorway, his leather vest revealing his heavily tattooed arms and black T-shirt. The classroom fell silent. My dad summoned the teacher with his index finger, and through gritted teeth, he commanded: 'Get here now.'

Fear across his face – a fear I recognised, as I saw it in the mirror each day before school – the teacher followed Dad out of the classroom, closing the door behind him, but not before I heard Dad say, 'I'm Trent's father,' and the teacher begin to stutter.

The kids stared at me. Not to bully me, but to simply look at me, wide-eyed. Dad, an Aboriginal man who was once a homeless teen with low hopes, can strike fear into anybody. At sixty-one years of age, he still commands the attention to part crowds. There is something about his presence that people feel. He has seen the ugliness of life and is unafraid of confrontation.

That day, he came and got me, gave me a hug and checked in on me. I witnessed a tenderness reserved for his loved ones, but I also knew that I was a vulnerable point for him. To be a vulnerable point for a man raised by the streets is terrifying, but also showcases the power of love.

—

The days that followed the incident were full of silence. I now got a seat on the bus and was left alone. My ultimate dream. I received handwritten apologies from the kids involved. I showed them to my parents, who encouraged my control over the situation. I could write responses back and have a mediation. I had the notes folded in my bag and took them out one afternoon. I sat with my back against my bedroom door, my face hot again as I relived the moment of shame and embarrassment. My parents had taught me that an apology was something you gave if there was an accident. This situation wasn't an accident, though. It was a deliberate attempt to cause pain for entertainment. I took delight in tearing up the handwritten apologies. They held no validity for me.

My thoughts on apologies shifted that day. If you've intentionally hurt someone, sit with that. Embrace it. Learn from it. Having a First Nations background, I'm uninterested in apologies. I want results. From that moment, I refused to be anyone's rehabilitation centre.

—

I had once yearned for a more conventional childhood, with parents who wore suits and a home that was enclosed by a white picket fence. A childhood filled with glorious holidays to places like Disneyland, and with time spent carelessly surfing the waves. We would be that perfect family you see on TV game shows. Those really wholesome types with wide grins and perfect looks.

I no longer yearned for such things. I saw my parents as my true heroes. I no longer wanted them to conform to the generic standards of society. I was proud. There was no more shame left in me. I was proud that they were different. I was proud to be different. I saw that being normal didn't pay off and I stopped wishing for that life. I'd later learn that board games just took up valuable luggage space in cars, and white picket fences were used to contain and conceal secrets. When trying to create the perfect, you miss out on the beauty and lessons of reality.

I look back at the desires of my early years and think 'how fucking boring' but, as a kid, all you want to do is fit in. Be normal. Go unnoticed. I didn't fully understand why I was such a target or why the advice from the school was to ignore it, as the bullies would move onto another target. This was an unacceptable response, but I'm grateful for it because that early exposure to ignorance allowed me to promise myself I'd never ignore such behaviour. I'd shine a light on it to protect others.

The strength that comes from being diverse is what deepens our humanity. It prepares us for unimaginable things, both good and bad. The tough moments in our life, of which I would have plenty afterwards, build our characters. Because of my initial struggles, I was equipped to take on future challenges in my personal and professional life. Adversity became my friend – it was something I could rely on as always being there to provide me with lessons. Those who positively change the world have not led regular lives. They too were once 'fucking weird' and that weirdness is now celebrated.

My loves, embrace your uniqueness. You will be celebrated one day.

EXOTIC BIRDS

TANIA OGIER

My mother was an exotic island bird, captured by my Australian father on the island of Savaii, Western Samoa, in 1969. Dad gently took Mum's hand from her mama and papa, led her out of the family fale, past ten siblings, across the green plantation and away from the village of her childhood. Humid golden curls sticking to the nape of his neck, the young adventurer lovingly flew his exotic island bird back to the civilisation of a three-bed, orange-brick bungalow, situated under the Tullamarine flightpath yet conveniently close to all amenities. For a while, the household I was brought home to when I was born had both parents present. The charming traveller who gashed his knee after falling partway down a Savaii volcano and the trainee nurse who tended to him were still very much in love. By day, Dad was a printing estimator but on weekends he enjoyed running miniature trains around a track he had built in the roof. Or indulging his passion for photography.

Occasionally he used the family caravan as a darkroom – I remember the smell of developing chemicals, and hundreds of rolls of negatives and contact sheets strewn around the cabin. My father usually shot weddings, but there were always glamorous photos of Mum in there somewhere, 'just to finish off the roll of film'. I can still see my mother's reflection staring provocatively from a gold baroque mirror as she stood in our tiny entrance hall, the walls lined with floral paper. Memories of this time are like seeing slivers of bright blue in an overcast sky. Almost as soon as the memory comes, it goes again, sometimes without sufficient time to either see or feel it fully.

As time went on, Mum got to know the local community and finally discovered the wonders of selling Avon cosmetics. She would stride down every street in the local area – without a shadow of doubt she was Avon's latest, fiercest entrepreneur. In one hand she'd hold a customer order, pinched shut between long red fingernails. Her other hand would be guiding my hefty pram along the footpath. The sight of my plump, dimpled legs kicking out from inside the moving carriage would set most of the local housewives on a squealing spending spree. I could bump up those musk perfume orders like nobody else. My mother knew and enjoyed that she looked 'different' to most of the women in her new community – in fact, standing out often worked to her advantage. She was extremely proud of her culture, without wanting it to completely define her. Mum was not naive; she was growing quickly and steadily more independent than ever before.

Moments before an Avon run one Saturday afternoon, Mum had a row with Dad in the backyard. His demands for a hot lunch were eventually met with her throwing a plateful of meat pie and sauce down the front of his shirt. Feeling mixed amounts of glee and panic, she ran back inside the kitchen – oven still on – to replace the spoiled pie with another. Dad was exasperated, hungry and red-faced from both sun and anger. 'Where are you going now?'

'I promised Carol I'd drop these off before two o'clock. Keep an eye on the oven!' Mum simultaneously gathered her beauty products and six-month-old me up in her arms.

—

The day my parents brought my baby sister home from the hospital I was two-and-a-half years old. I sat on the front brick fence of my grandparents' house with a posy of garden flowers clenched in my waiting fist.

My sister was tiny, red and sleeping. I pinched her through her crochet suit when nobody was looking, just to see if I could wake her. I don't remember much else about the first two or three years of her life.

The separation of not only my parents, but of myself from my younger sister – whom my mother took as part of their divorce arrangement – made an indelible impression on my formative years. Not only was I navigating my burgeoning identity in an era when mixed heritage was still considered different, but I was also being raised by a single father, who everyone told me I little resembled. This at times felt like a double whammy of shame. Meanwhile, my mother forged ahead with life post-divorce and her growing entrepreneurial spirit knew few bounds. I was both in awe of and confounded by her, she was feisty yet always loving, often flighty and seemingly infallible.

—

I lingered awkwardly at the Ansett arrivals gate at Coolangatta airport, wearing an unaccompanied-flyer badge and waiting to be collected. My school holidays were different from my sister's, as we now lived in different states. I still had a week to float around in the pool before the Queensland school term was over and we could go to the opening of Dreamworld. The long-sleeved dress Nanna put me in early that morning in Melbourne had not translated well to the afternoon heat. Nanna had also curled my hair in rags the previous night, after I begged her to give me ringlets like Laura from *Little House on the Prairie*. Today I just looked like a Polynesian Pollyanna – I even had to wave both arms when I spotted Mum approaching, as she didn't recognise me.

My mother hugged me tightly and it seemed to go on forever. In the moment, I realised how much I missed her energy, her mum smell, the familiarity of embracing another who looked like me. It was instant acceptance, acceptance I had neither to wish nor work for. It wasn't that I didn't appreciate my father's love, or the love of my doting grandparents in Melbourne. It's just that there's nothing like strutting around alongside the strong, beautiful woman you are from. Nobody asks if you're adopted, there are no sideways glances. It's obvious to everyone that you are family.

After my hug, Mum looked me up and down, grabbed at my hair, my buttons – her smile didn't slip. About an hour later I was wandering around a shopping centre, carrying shopping bags and wearing a completely new outfit.

I adored lazing around whichever house Mum was living in at the time. Almost every year it changed; however, the houses were always much nicer than our orange bungalow in Tullamarine. I ran around in my bathers all day, stole biscuits from the pantry and made my new baby brother laugh, just so I could poke his dimples.

Sometimes my aunties were there at the same time – a gaggle of simultaneously beautiful and terrifying women. I loved the attention, the laughter, the uproarious conversations in both English and a language I didn't understand. I smiled as if I followed what they were saying, only to get a playful shove in the head in return, or an exaggerated kiss on the cheek. The physicality of Samoan expression and the spirited closeness of family was something I wasn't used to, yet I felt it was a way of being that I partially belonged to.

One afternoon after school, I saw my sister get off the school bus and run towards the house in tears. She raced through the front door and straight to the bathroom, pulling up her blue-checked school uniform as she went. She was sobbing.

'What the hell is going on, Miss Muffet?' My mother's voice was shrill as she banged on the door in a panic. She entered to find her younger daughter coating herself in baby powder.

'I wish I was white!'

—

'I'll drop you at the bus stop today,' Mum said quietly. That was an order, not an offer.

'No! Let me walk,' was my sister's futile response.

Mum left the engine running, with me in the passenger seat. She prised my sister out from the back and across into the waiting school bus. I sat holding my breath, waiting for the bus to burst into flames. At least we'll be at Dreamworld tomorrow, I said over and over in my head. The next five minutes felt like twenty. Finally, my mother alighted the bus, clopping down the steps in her linen dress like a dusky Lady Diana stepping off a private jet. She returned to the car amid a cloud of Estée Lauder perfume and victory.

'Was she there? That mean girl that sits at the back?' My eyes were wide.

'Oh, I told that little shit.'

—

We were dancing on a floating restaurant as it made its fairy-lit way up the Noosa River. My sister and I were not dancing as guests, instead we were part of the after-dinner floor show. Mum's usual dancers had called in sick again.

'Hungover, more like it,' she muttered, eyeing us as we crammed ourselves into grass skirts in the tiny toilet stall.

The island-themed restaurant was our mother's domain, for as long as she and our new stepfather owned and ran it. Ever the entrepreneur, Mum gave anything her all, including folding napkins into perfect swans to place on each dinner table.

That evening, in the absence of paid performers, my sister and I were it. I hated trying to dance the Samoan siva because I'd never learned how. Who was supposed to teach me? My Australian father or my arthritic Irish nanna? My old English pa? Despite this I smiled, swaying my non-existent pre-teen hips and doing movements with my hands that I prayed looked convincing. Our mother was the star, anyway – all grace and glowing skin, moving with confidence. My sister and I were just her ducklings, unsure and wobbling in the background. The best we could hope for was a mention in the guest book and a glass of watered-down Coke from the bar afterwards.

—

The flight home was always awful. I would cry at the loss of my mother all over again. Shuffling off the plane at Tullamarine in a hot-pink terry-towelling jumpsuit with my hair in plaits, I looked so cute yet felt so sad. Dad was already there, arms open wide, his smile flecked with gold as it always was. I found hollow comfort in his arms, still couldn't stop crying.

'My god, you're as brown as a peanut!' he declared. Dad always said the same thing when I returned after summer holidays. I did miss him. So much. He only had to mention that the cat had had kittens while I was away, or that one of my friends wanted to come round for tea and I knew I was back. We made our way home, via Nanna's first for roast lamb and apple pie, then back to the orange bungalow and our exotic lives.

FISH PEOPLE

MIRANDA JAKICH

I have seen enough fish heads to fill the deepest ocean. And smelt like one too. Have even imagined I came from the bottom of the sea. Not a mermaid whose tangled tresses were knotted with seaweed, her tail shimmering, but a scaly, slippery snapper with its head cut off by my father.

My father could hack off fish heads with a single strike. I'd watch, recoiling as their glittering guts spilt onto the bench before trickling over to splash at my feet. He would run, too, from the back shed to the shopfront, carrying crates of fish, his lips pursed, before tossing them down with a grunt. In his reddened hands, they changed from slippery fish with glazed eyes to neatly skinned fillets. Then my mother fried them golden and sprayed them generously with salt, ready to feed the mouths that queued outside.

'Givvus two lots of fish 'n' chips, mate. Lots of vinegar. And chuck in some tomato sauce for the missus.'

'Tenk you, tenk you.' My mother's voice competing against the rustling of paper and hissing oil vats as she struggled with customers' orders.

'Faster, faster.' My father's voice, impatient as he flung cooked fish her way. 'Use your head, woman. Where's that child? We need her to hold them back at the door.'

Grease clung to the air around us. Even though my mother poured bottles of perfume over us and saturated our clothes, still we reeked. The smell of fish stuck to us like an old, inseparable friend. Just like the families who spent Sunday evenings with us. We were a tribe of fish people, familiar and safe with each other, strange to the englezi around us. 'Smelly foreigners ... Dad says foreigners all stink.'

'Fish smell, fish smell ... Mum says you sleep in a fish crate.'

Black eyes, torn dress, daily fist fights defending my family's honour. Such exhausting work being the child of fish people.

'You're not a girl, you're worse than a boy,' my mother despaired. 'Nobody will marry you when you grow up. You and this curse of a country will send me to an early grave.'

'But they say bad things about us. I can't let them.'

'They say we're forners?'

'Foreigners, Dad. It's foreigners.'

'Don't you tell me how to speak the language! Out the back before I kick you so far you'll go flying over the roof,' my father bellowed, his face like a snapper's in boiling water.

Cradled by fish boxes, I would plot revenge on my persecutors at school. I closed my eyes and the teachers were awarding me a prize for best student, then I was a ballerina, spinning on pointes, acclaimed and famous. They threw roses onto the stage. Better still, I was an author and the teachers said, 'We could see it from the start. She was too good for our town.'

My father would come out, crazy with stress, and summon me inside. Smelling like a toxic pond, I would go in, dizzy from the promise of a beautiful future where englezi adored me. I knew then it would not be fish forever.

—

A fish child knows all about being alone.

'Where are our family?' I asked.

My father's face grew dark, his eyes like shrunken olives, cheekbones jutting like knives ready to cut. 'You have us and that's all you'll ever need.'

But somehow they were always with us, smiling in photographs in the suitcase under my parents' bed, strong Slavic cheekbones rising towards hypnotic eyes. They were mere sepia portraits but I longed for them. Maybe they would appear in the flesh one day when I grew up and the whole world knew about me.

—

Sundays were bliss. My mother would wake us with her Mario Lanza record that always made her cry. The freezer doors were bolted, the shop hosed down. I would hurry through my list of morning chores, cutting piles of newspaper for Monday, dusting the mounted varnished lobster that hung in the shop. Dad would listen to the World Cup and holler when Yugoslavia scored. My mother would sew new dresses to replace the ones ripped in battle. In the summer we jumped into our Plymouth and joined other fish families on the beach with our bulging picnic hampers full of ham, salami, pastries and thick black coffee. My mother would show the other women the veins spreading on her legs.

'From standing in the shop all day,' she complained. They purred in sympathy and checked out their own legs. I would read aloud from magazines in our language and the women would dab their eyes. My father, though, would sit unsmiling, refusing to swim in the sea.

Behind Elvis Presley sunglasses, I knew his eyes were disapproving.

'There is no sea like our beautiful Adriatic,' he ruled.

—

Once a year my parents dressed in sequins and lace to celebrate National Day. Like glamorous movie stars with champagne smiles, they swirled around the floor, dancing shoes on their gumboot feet, satin gloves concealing my mother's worn hands. They exchanged nostalgic memories under the portraits of the Queen and President Tito.

'Our takings were up this year,' my father told friends. 'We should have a down payment on a house soon.' So proud to be making a good living selling fish. Life wasn't that bad in the new country after all.

—

My mother had wrapped her stilettos and sequined frock in tissue and mothballs. She wouldn't need them until the next National

Day. Again she wore her apron, plastic arm protectors and solid shoes that raised her off the concrete floor – the cause of her treescape of leg veins.

'I never asked to come here and work like a slave. I hate this country. I want to go home!' she wailed.

'Go back! Nobody goes back! You were hungry over there. What do you have to be unhappy about now?' Brutal words from my father.

'Unhappy! Of course I'm unhappy! I'm just a slave feeding fish to englezi!'

Their voices mingled with the cries of prowling cats. Cats that stalked our shed howling for the thrill of fish between their teeth. I implored God to help people like us, lost at the bottom of the world.

'Dear God, make them stop and say they love each other. And let all those kids at school fall into a big hole and get eaten alive by snapping turtles.'

—

Screams from my mother while frying fish. My father carried her out in a dead faint and the ambulance took her away. Would I be left alone with just my father and dead fish? Forever without a mother. But she came back from hospital, her arm in a bandage. Exhausted from going fish, batter, dip, oil, fish, batter, dip, oil, she told me her hand had slipped into the boiling cooker. She had been distracted by her dream of returning to the village and seeing her mother.

Girlhood had been simple, bound by fig trees, vineyards and

orange groves where the fruit grew puffy and sweet. My father swept in – a bigshot who had made money abroad and come back for a bride. He swaggered into the village wearing stylish foreign clothes, sunnies perched on high cheekbones, cheekbones to die for. A swashbuckling, silver-tongued charmer who conjured up a land of plenty, even as he was conflicted about this new country that did not seem to want him or his ideas.

I sat by my mother's bed as she recovered and listened to her talk about the bleached mountains and how she would shake the olive boughs and watch the ripe olives rain down. She relived her wedding day, naming all the guests and how they were related to us. It was a wedding without priests, and the piano accordion played until dawn. They saluted Tito with small brandy glasses and thought they were the luckiest people in the world.

'Everyone said we looked like those people in American magazines, you know, like movie stars.'

He built a house under the Biokovo mountain range so she could be first in the village to see the sunrise. From their bedroom window they looked down to the endless blue where fishing boats floated. 'People said I was the happiest girl in the village and they could hear my laugh across the olive groves.'

Then she fell pregnant and my father changed his mind. He said the child would have a better life on the other side of the world. So capitalism can't be that bad, the villagers mused. My mother felt confused and betrayed but was duty-bound to follow her husband. Her own mother rested her hand on her daughter's belly and lamented that she would not see her unborn grandchild. The old fortune-teller crossed herself and warned them not to stay away for long. 'They make money but God always takes something away. Their minds flap in the wind, braying about success but making less sense than my donkey.'

A singing procession escorted them out of the village. My father held my mother as she wept and stumbled against the stones. Village girls threw oleander petals over her hair and wished her good fortune in the new land. The old women touched her for the last time, saying they would be in their grave before her return. An old hag rustled her petticoats, opened her toothless mouth and screeched, 'God protect you from the devils that live in Amerika.' Every place outside her village was Amerika. No-one thought to correct her so her curses could fall where they should.

They journeyed while her insides burned, and the child was delivered in Australia in a miasma of trauma and fear. She looked around her poky bedroom, alone with her fiery husband and fish child, and instead of orange groves out the window she saw a highway with trucks spewing gas. Instead of olives thumping to the ground, she heard the dull thud of fish crates as the week's supply was unloaded. A few weeks later she was back on the production line, feeding fish to the world and hating it.

My mother was always crying after that burn to her arm. If I brought her a bowl of fruit she would weep, remembering the wild cherries that grew along the Dalmatian coast. If I accidentally spoke English she would wring her hands. Even though I promised to become a perfect fish child, obedient and devoted, she never let go of the fear that englezi were lining up to abduct me.

———

A million reeking fish crates (and nine years) later, my mother finally breaks. Her face appears above me, pale as the flesh of a dead fish. She has her wild, black-eyed look. Her voice is a strangled whimper.

'Tell your father we're leaving.'

'Where are we going? To see grandmother in the village?'

But she just stands there in her street clothes and sobs, looking helplessly at the door.

We never went anywhere. That night we sat in silence. Outside, the corrugated iron on the tin shed twanged in the wind. It seemed to be taunting us, the fish people hoodwinked by the promise of a better life. Inside the shed the fish lay bunked down for the night, their smell curling out through the cracks in the iron to send most of the local cats into moonlight madness.

My father had wiped his dripping boots and stood them by the door ready for the next day. He sat smoking and flicked the occasional fish scale off his trouser leg. I counted out the small coins from the day's takings and put them into neat piles.

My mother bent over my head. She looked at the wall, flecks of pain in her eyes.

'This child smells like a fish no matter what I do.'

I would try harder to make her happy and to look over at my father, not the wall. And every morning I would secretly rub her perfume onto my skin so she could imagine herself back in the village among the oleander trees and forget she was fenced in with fish.

DIE HARD

BON-WAI CHOU

At twenty-one I was terrified of her. I would stay overnight at her place, scared stiff of the unpredictable morning.

'Wake up! D'you hear me? Wake up!'

My grandmother was bending over me in a greasy apron, shaking a fierce finger at me. She had ripped off the bedcovers.

'Paw! Only low-class girls sleep naked!'

I frowned, unable to understand the turn my dream had taken.

'Did you hear what I said? *Get up*. We're going back to Collins Street to get my hearing aid fixed.'

Pulling the bedcovers up around my neck, I grunted and rolled over to retrieve the pleasures of my early-morning dreams.

'And I need to get something for Joyce's dog!'

I said something indistinctly and went back to sleep. I don't know how long it took before I nerved myself and jumped out of bed.

'Oh my God,' I said, pulling back the curtains and waking properly. The memory of previous visits to town surfaced with a kind of revulsion. 'Oh my God,' I repeated. 'I can't stomach any more of this!'

I felt as if I was descending down a precipice when I put the car in gear.

'Gee, look at you! Greasy hair! Rickety ribs! It's beyond me why *anyone* would want to go round looking like a beggar!'

I pressed my foot on the pedal and the car shot down the road.

'How about "Good morning. How are you?"' I said coldly.

'*How are you!* Why do I need to ask? Look at you with your sour face! I know how you are. In a bad mood, as usual.'

'What do you expect when I have to take you into town every week to fix your hearing aid?'

'Is it my fault if they never fix it right?'

—

At the audiologist's, my grandmother told the receptionist the familiar story of her faulty hearing aid while I listened with a surly expression. The door marked PRIVATE opened and a portly, cheerful middle-aged man appeared.

'Docta!' My grandmother sprang on him. 'No fix-ee right! Sound ringing awla time!'

Dr Goodwin's smile disappeared. He took the hearing aid from my grandmother's bony hand. 'Now let me see,' he said, turning the tiny contraption over several times. 'I'd better check with the technician.' As he went back through the door marked PRIVATE, my grandmother spoke to me in Cantonese.

'Don't like the look of him.'

'Don't start that again—'

'Eyes too close together. A bad egg, if you ask me. He obviously doesn't like us Chinese.'

The door swung open and Dr Goodwin reappeared.

'Mrs Chun-Tie, a tiny electronic part has snapped off. We can fix it right away for forty dollars, if you like.'

'Can't hear,' said my grandmother, eyeing him furiously.

I told my grandmother the price.

'*What?* Forty dollars? It should be free!'

'We're actually helping you save money by fixing it,' said Dr Goodwin. 'A new hearing aid will set you back one thousand and eighty-three dollars.'

'You say new hearing aid *free?*'

Dr Goodwin turned to me. 'Tell your grandmother I'll give her a discount.'

My grandmother said, 'You give me *free?*'

'It's a specialised, handmade piece,' Dr Goodwin continued. 'The latest technology.' He plunged into technicalities and my grandmother flared up.

'Paw! I know teck-nology! Makes everything more cheap more better! Twenty dollars I pay for cleaning build-up of wax last week. Thirty dollars I pay for broken wire. Now forty dollars. This is no teck-nology. It's daylight robbery!' she growled half in Cantonese, half in English.

'I can give you a new hearing aid but certain conditions apply—'

'Can't hear. Speak up!'

I grabbed my grandmother's arm.

'Just pay the forty dollars.'

'Thirty-five!' she said in Cantonese.

'Por-Por, stop it.'

'You're too much logic!'

'You're unreasonable.'

'I think above reasoning!'

'Look, we haven't got all day. Remember Joyce's dog? C'mon.'

When the hearing aid disappeared once again behind the door marked PRIVATE, my grandmother trembled with silent rage. After selecting the most crumpled notes from her purse, she then counted out the grubbiest coins. When Dr Goodwin reappeared with the hearing aid, she plonked down the money, casting him the evil eye.

'Daylight robbery!' she kept saying, as I edged her out the door.

We went up Collins Street, turned into Swanston then crossed Bourke Street and all the time my grandmother kept repeating, 'Paw! Daylight robbery, I tell you! Daylight robbery!' Passers-by stared at her gibbering away. Some burst out laughing.

I was afraid for my grandmother and worried she was going mad. I thought about the dire events of her past, the blows in her life, the unceasing bombardment of her identity. As a teenage bride in Townsville, vicious *gwei* louts pelted eggs and stones at her mixed-grocery business. Then, during the Depression, some of the very people who'd bludgeoned her and reduced her status were now entirely without food and thronging to her shop. She found crusts of bread and provisions for everyone. But she would have been disturbed when the American troops stationed in Townsville during World War II furthered the assault on her boundaries by stealing her pet bulldog to take to New Guinea as their mascot.

God knows how my grandmother lived through her only son dying at twenty-one, and the death of her husband six months later. That was a torture that tried even me, for I absorbed from birth her frenzied howling and unreconciled confusion.

My grandmother was still protesting when we entered a newly opened souvenir store in Chinatown. No sooner had I run my hand through a super-soft sheepskin rug, thinking it would be nice for Joyce's dog, than she barked, 'Paw! You know how much these things cost?'

We came out onto the street again. My grandmother's gimlet eye caught a shop window hung with red lanterns.

'Where are you going?' I asked.

She didn't answer. She was already hobbling across the road. The shelves in the long, narrow room were heaped with strange and splendid treasures – captivating tea sets, silk cushion covers, gold-painted fans, and fat buddhas and goddesses clasping lotus flowers and strings of beads.

'Humph! All the usual stuff,' said my grandmother.

I inhaled the exotic mix of incense, wood and paper.

'Oh, this is *perfect*,' I cried, catching sight of an urn covered with a flat lid and painted in the most enchanting colours – pastel pink, purple, yellow, emerald green.

The next moment my grandmother had grabbed the urn in her bony hands.

'What? This cheap-looking thing,' she said, turning it 360 degrees. 'Nothing special at all!'

'It's beautiful.'

She exploded. 'Paw! What you want an urn for!'

I shrugged and cast down my eyes. 'Ornament,' I said.

This provoked a fresh torrent.

'Gawd, Mei-Mei, you're nothing but an idiot. Throwing your money away!'

'Not so loud,' I said, clutching the urn and indicating the balding shopkeeper absorbed in the *Australian Chinese Daily*.

'You'll get ripped off! Let me handle this.'

My grandmother was wresting the urn back from me when a voice came from the shadows.

'Careful, you'll break it.'

'How much?' my grandmother barked.

'Sixty dollars.'

'*Sixty dollars?* You can't be serious!'

'Tie-Tie,' said the man slowly, putting away his newspaper. 'Sixty dollars is a very good price for a genuine hand-crafted product.'

'This cheap old thing! You can get these rough old things in Guangzhou for no more than ten *renminbi!*'

I clutched my head. 'Por-Por, *please—*'

'C'mon! Forty dollar! Take it or leave it.'

'*Ai ya*, Tie-Tie. No bargaining, please. We're in Australia.'

'Look at the workmanship!' she shot back. 'The glaze is totally missing in this part! See how thick is the rim? Talk about shoddy and *crude*.'

'But culturally significant,' said the shopkeeper. 'From Peking.'

'So what? The best porcelain is from Zhen-de-jing.'

'Por-Por, *please*,' I pleaded. My grandmother didn't have any idea what she was talking about. China's porcelain capital is Jingdezhen.

'*Ai ya*, Tie-Tie. I have a family to feed.'

My grandmother opened her purse, fished out three blue notes and a purple one. 'There,' she said, placing the money on the counter with a gesture of finality. 'Thirty-five dollar! You're making good money on this!'

'Por-Por! That's—'

'Thirty-five!' she repeated, signalling me to be quiet.

'Tie-Tie, you know I'm losing on this.'

'Paw! Business is business! Come on, let's finish it. Thirty-five dollar!' She eyed the shopkeeper. 'Look, my neighbour's dog is dying. She needs a nice container to keep his ashes.' She tapped on the money impatiently. 'Take it or leave it.'

The man looked at the crisp notes, razor-sharp, and snatched them from the counter.

'I knew you'll do it! That's business! Just think, if it wasn't for us that urn would still be sitting on the shelf gathering dust.' She softened her voice. 'Please do me the favour of wrapping the urn in lots of paper. Wrap the lid separately. We'll need a box, too. A nice strong one. Yes, that one. Tie it up with string, please. We're catching the bus home and have a long way to go. Don't want anything broken, after all this trouble …'

At last we walked out. I carried the large box, frowning. After a moment, my grandmother said: 'Paw! Why the long face? I bought the urn for you, stupid. It's nearly your birthday, isn't it? I wanted a strong box to give to Joyce because Kye loves cardboard boxes more than anything. He would much prefer to lie and stretch out on cardboard than on a mat!'

I stared at her.

My grandmother beamed.

'I tell you, I have cutting-edge teck-nology! My ideas come to me like gifts! Like magnets!' She kept walking, a glint in her eye. 'By gee, that piece of cardboard saved me five dollars eighty. Time and petrol all in. I tell you, I'm always lucky! Wealth comes like magic!'

Lucky or crazy, this hysterical woman haunted and terrorised me. The turmoil of her emotions made my life miserable. Yet it was obvious within a few minutes of meeting her she had a dazzling, indestructible power. Like diamonds created under pressure, the hideous turmoil and overwhelming agitations *became* her.

I had no real conception as to why she choked herself up with struggles. In her later years, there was more than enough money but she lived like it was hard-going. She panicked over a few cents and people ran when they saw her coming. Her deranged outbursts, exaggerated rage, despotic faith, simplicity and scoundrel artistry confused me with shame, curiosity and fascination.

She never seemed to give up. All her strains of perplexity intrigued me long after she'd gone. I came to see I was privileged to enter her world of underworld guile, between-worlds chatter, refined fiction and invention I could never forget.

She would never have known she was an artist, and I never knew that I'd met my muse until after she was gone.

LEARNING HOW TO DO SPORT

PRATEETI SABHLOK

My legs bounce as Mum drives into the carpark. I'd been watching the white lines on the road long enough to get dizzy, but now I see kids running with their bags thumping against their backs.

When we find a parking spot, Mum turns the radio off. I don't get it, but she says not hearing noise makes her see better when she parks.

I open the door as soon as she pulls the car keys out. I nearly start running like the other kids. The girl on the website had been so pretty, and I can't wait to be pretty just like her.

Finally, I'll be trying synchronised swimming!

Last term, I was meant to try it for the first time. But Mum doesn't know the area very well, and the pool is in a big school. By the time we got there it was dark. It looked like the buildings were going to bed. The lights in the windows were gone, and I thought someone was going to come and tell us that we had to leave or we'd be stuck in there forever.

When we finally found the pool, I couldn't join because we were too late. But the teacher let us watch some of the older girls training. They'd done a whole lap on their backs, looking at the ceiling, with their right legs straight in the air.

I don't think I'll ever be able to do that.

I grab my swimming bag from the back seat. Mum packed it for me, everything in different plastic bags. I've got my favourite goggles and I'm wearing my favourite brown pants.

The car door on Mum's side slams shut. She makes a clicking sound when she checks the watch on her wrist. I already know we're late (as usual).

We start walking fast. The pool is at the bottom of a hill, with bushes lining the path on both sides. A bunch of kids with their parents trailing behind them are going the same direction as us. I can see movement through the windows of the buildings, and all the lights are on. Now we know how to get to the pool, the buildings look like they're wide awake and up for a chat.

I pull a leaf off a bush as we walk and pick at it until only half is left. I wonder who's going to be there. Will they be like the older girls I saw? I bet they're all really good.

I start feeling like I ate something bad.

I stop walking. Mum doesn't notice. I don't want to be left behind, but I don't want to keep going down to the pool either.

I've just realised something, but I don't know how to say it. It feels like I've waited the fifteen minutes before the school bell rings and I'm watching the clock tick-tick-tick before Mum slows down and turns around. She looks at me standing still. 'What are you doing?'

I kind of know before I even say it that Mum's going to be angry.

'I don't want to do it anymore. Let's go home.' I try my best to sound like I have a real reason, while looking down at what's left of the leaf.

'What?' Mum looks confused.

'I don't want to do it.'

'Why not?'

'I don't know.' I want to walk into the bushes lined up against the path with all their little leaves and hide.

Mum doesn't say anything for a while. It looks like she's thinking.

'Well, I've already paid for the full term. You have to go.'

The sick feeling in my stomach gets worse. I look down at my feet instead of the bushes and force myself to move.

My chest starts to feel smaller and smaller, like I can't relax. Something is going to go bad. But I don't know how to say no again. Mum already paid, and Dad keeps talking about how money doesn't grow on trees.

We go through two sets of big glass doors and enter the pool. The place is hot. And loud. There are a bunch of people in the lap lanes swimming. A coach is yelling. A boy makes a big splash after diving.

I keep following Mum and don't stop this time.

I'm still looking around and don't even realise when we arrive at the synchronised swimming class. A tall lady with brunette hair in a ponytail smiles down at me. 'Hello, I'm Jess, what's your name?'

Just behind her, there are some kids sitting on mats. They have their legs out and are bending forward to touch their toes.

'Prateeti,' I reply.

'Pra-tee-ti? Is that right?' Jess says. I nod. 'Alright, well, let's get to stretching. Next time, make sure you wear something you can exercise in. Those brown pants don't look like they have much stretch.'

I frown and look down at my pants. I can't wear my favourite brown pants?

Jess teaches me some stretching, and I try to touch my toes too. Once we hop into the pool, I get shown how to do a tub. I have to lie on my back and look at the roof. Then with my hands by my side – it's called sculling – I bring my knees to my face on the surface of the water.

When she teaches me how to spin in a tub, I immediately know this is the sport for me. I feel like the pretty girl on the website. I love synchronised swimming.

—

I love synchronised swimming, but sometimes I wish Mum knew about shaving and waxing like the other girls.

We're lining up in our bathers to get in the pool. All I can think about is how my thighs are bigger than everyone else's and my legs are hairier than everyone else's too. As soon as the coach tells us what to do, I'm first to get in the pool.

No-one can see what you look like under the water.

'Two laps eggbeater with both arms up, and one lap support scull, let's go!'

We've finished our swimming warm-up and we are doing skills now. I'm tired from primary school, but I put my nose clip on and get ready.

I start the eggbeater, lifting both my arms but keeping them forward. My legs are treading water and I'm moving upright through the water for twenty-five metres. 'Shoulders back, Prateeti!' the coach yells.

I ignore her. I don't usually ignore the coach but there's something I don't want anyone else to see. There's no way I'm bringing my arms all the way up. She yells the same thing again and I shift my arms slightly, but not all the way back.

We move on to verticals on the wall. We all get ready, bringing our legs out of the water and resting them on the pool grate.

We're waiting for the coach to find her spoon and start tapping on the wall, then we will go upside down. With the spoon, we can hear the tapping underwater and hold it for ten counts.

Kristina and Maya, two of my teammates, are chatting about how much homework they have. Maya glances at my legs on the grate.

'My mum always waxes my legs,' she says loudly.

'Doesn't it hurt?' Kristina says.

'It does, but then the hair doesn't grow back thicker.'

Finally, the coach has found the spoon. She starts shouting again. 'Everyone ready? And, under!'

I dunk my head underwater and look at the lines between the tiles as we hold our upside-down vertical position. My face is burning. I don't know anything about waxing or how hair grows back thicker.

Later on, in the change rooms, I'm drying my arms off when another one of my teammates, Sarah, looks at me. 'What's the weird curly thing under your arms?'

'What?' My arms aren't dry yet but I don't care right now. I grab my shirt and put it on.

Sarah goes on. 'It looks so funny, what is it?'

I don't know what to say. The dampness of my arms is clinging to the fabric of the shirt. I'd tried to hide it. I'd always avoided lifting my arms in training and had let myself be yelled at by the coach for bad posture.

I'd also tried to pretend it was all in my head and that no-one cared.

Maya butts in. 'It's just some hair, you'll have it too one day.'

Maya is so lucky to know about all this stuff already.

'Eww, will I? It looks so weird, though.' Sarah looks genuinely confused, and the other girls laugh.

I quickly finish putting my clothes on and run to the car.

At home, I sneak into my parents' bathroom and steal a new shaver from under the sink. I don't care what Mum says, I'm shaving everything off. I shave my face, my arms and my legs. I don't care that I accidentally make some small cuts that hurt.

—

I love synchronised swimming, but sometimes I wish Mum knew what girls are supposed to do to make sure they can swim all the time.

I have my period. And we have a competition today.

I'm stressing. Mum is stressing. I usually skip training when I have my period, or Mum puts pads in the liner of my bathers. But I made her stop when my teammates said there was white fluff appearing in the pool.

It's the first day of my period so maybe it won't be that bad. We drive to the competition.

We are late and I know my coach is going to ask why. I'll just say I don't know, as usual.

We have to get our hair and make-up done. The coaches help me pull my thick, curly hair into a bun. It hurts a lot but I squeeze my eyes shut and count in my head. They help me do eyeshadow and I learn how to do mascara. They say the eyeshadow looks good on my skin. I leave it until the last minute to change into my bathers and take my pad off.

The competition starts with a figure competition where we have to do specific synchronised movements in front of the judges. We have four to do and we all wear black bathers and white swimming caps.

I'm not so nervous for my first figure, and I think I do okay. I get out of the pool and walk to the end of the queue. I start talking to Sarah about the next figure – 'I hate doing the spin' – when Sarah gasps and points at my legs. 'Are you okay? You're bleeding!'

I look down. There's blood running down my legs. 'It's okay!' I quickly say without thinking.

'It looks really bad, though!' Sarah looks like she is about to go tell someone.

'It's fine! I'll just go sit down.' I skip the queue, weave between lots of girls getting ready to compete, and sit in the water at the edge of the pool.

I watch the water wash the blood away.

My shoulders are tensing and Sarah comes over. She still looks worried. 'Are you sure?' she says.

'It's fine! It's gone now,' I say. It's okay, it's okay, it's okay.

She stops asking about it and I stay sitting there until it's my turn again.

I make sure I sit on my towel as soon as we are finished. And I don't move, even when the coach wants to take group photos, until Mum comes to pick me up and everyone else has left. My eyes are watering as I stand up and the towel is covered in blood.

—

I'm walking down the path to training. I pick a few leaves from the bushes and start peeling them into halves.

It's been a long time since I went to my first synchronised swimming class.

I can't remember what the pretty girl on the website actually looked like anymore, but I can do more push-ups than any of the boys in my class, I can do the splits and I can put on eyeshadow.

Halfway to the pool, I check the time. Uh-oh. I'm late again.

I start running.

MEMORY DRIVE

AMER ETRI

'Ya Ummoh!' I called out from the top of the driveway. I knew Mum wouldn't hear me announcing my arrival from here because I still had the length of a short run-up and cricket pitch to go before I reached her usual location at this hour, but I did it anyway. This was our little game of echolocation. I'd keep calling her until she called, 'Ya Ummoh!' back and we pinpointed each other's position.

It was late afternoon and the heat and humidity had formed a hostile alliance with each other. There was nothing to signify the arrival of autumn except for a heap of dry leaves that rustled its way from one corner to another as it rode the warm breeze.

'Ya Ummoh!'

The fading red-stencilled driveway lay to the left of the burnt-orange brick house, which rose high above it. The garage-cum-granny flat that stood at the end of it – cement rendered and painted in Dulux Handmade Linen Half – was now reflecting the afternoon light, beckoning me towards it. When our century-old, weathered weatherboard childhood home was going to be torn down, the architect had tried to convince Dad to replace the driveway with an attached garage and extra living space. Dad refused, on the grounds that a driveway gave you access to the backyard and could fit seven cars instead of two. We, the children, weren't asked our opinion. We didn't care about the structure of the new house, beyond the basic request that it wouldn't wake us up in the middle of the night by laughingly leaking water onto our face when it rained. The scramble to get a bowl under the leak before our bed was soaked was one of the many charming challenges that helped forge our future selves.

'Ya Ummoh!'

No echo to greet me yet. I was embraced instead by the savoury combination of fried tomato, onion and garlic. I wasn't going to return home from this visit hungry today.

The path that I trod right now, from the street down to the back of my childhood home, was well worn. My parents first pulled into the driveway after co-purchasing the property in 1971, two years after leaving Lebanon. Raising three children under three years old in one bedroom of a share house in Sydney's Inner West was no longer viable. Ignoring the warnings of the few friends they had formed, they raised a home-loan deposit with a number of family members and moved out west, beyond the 'Strathfield Line' to what would become one of Australia's most ethnically diverse suburbs. My parents proudly played a role in making that happen by building the mandatory fibro appendage to the back of the original house and using it as a halfway home for the relatives whose migration from Lebanon they sponsored. Once they found their feet, and a few thousand dollars for a loan deposit, most of these new arrivals didn't move too far away. Two of them moved into the same street and still reside there, clinging onto their small cups of coffee and their sense of community as the sun sets on their golden years.

'Ya Ummoh!'

This rectangular space, original and rebuilt, carried the sum of my family's memories. It bore the cracks of countless comings and goings. It was from here my mother departed shrieking under the stress of labour pangs six times, and returned with a baby tightly swaddled in a blue or pink muslin wrap. The first of the new additions to the family arrived only a few metres away from the house, in the back seat of our neighbour Gloria's lime green Holden Kingswood. Not owning our own car at the time to transport Mum to the hospital, or possessing a telephone to call an ambulance, meant that number four of my siblings would forever be the most quintessential Aussie of the nine of us.

'Ya Ummoh!'

Dad might hear me before Mum. He had a habit of hiding from the sun in the shade of an overgrown cactus on the front balcony at this time of the day, watching the happenings of his shrinking world on the familiar street before him. There was a time, before the rebuild, I would hide in the shadows at the front of the house to avoid being noticed in the place most passers-by believed was abandoned because of its sorry state. Not many of my schoolfriends had come to appreciate the difference between a house and home, so I remained as inconspicuous as possible.

Dad wasn't on the balcony today.

I was about a third of the way down the driveway now. This was where the unmarked bowling crease used to lie. Spurred on by the summer cricket season, our neighbours would gather on the rock-hard pitch after the day's heat had started to ease, for as many overs that could be bowled before it was too dark to see the ball. Without a single piece of proper cricket equipment between us, we improvised. We used sticky tape to wrap a tennis ball and make it as firm as any six-stitcher Kookaburra could conjure up. Dairy Farmers proudly sponsored our wickets and supplied two maroon milk crates. Our bat was carefully crafted out of an old fence paling that had fallen off the sagging row at the back of the house. We cut the paling to resemble a handle, shoulder, middle, edge and toe. Being two-dimensional, it had no such thing as a sweet spot. Any contact with the speeding, stone-hard ball sent the batter shuddering. It was a good minute before you came to and learnt if you had hit the ball over the fence, which was a measly metre away from the wicket, and scored a six and out. Reports about the real game of cricket were called out from behind the torn flyscreen of the living-room window that opened onto the driveway. 'Boon's out!' our Aussie sister would disappointingly declare. Boony was our favourite. He was sturdy and stoic and knew how to drive a ball down the ground, the only way we could score on our pitch without getting out at the same time.

'Ya Ummoh!'

I guessed that Mum could hear me by now but was pretending

not to because she wanted me to get closer before she called back to me – she and Dad were probably having dinner.

Any ball hit over the short boundary fence to the right of the wicket would land in our Turkish neighbour's yard. Retrieving it was never a problem because the older of her two sons would usually be playing with us and we would send him off to fetch it. His mother had all the odds stacked against her; she was female, a non-White immigrant, a single mother and a paraplegic. Yet, after gaining her driver's licence and buying a modified car, she managed to provide me and two of my brothers with a refreshing escape from the reality of our overcrowded house by ferrying us off to fishing trips around Sydney Harbour, and on the only Macca's runs we ever did as children. We could never pay her back for her generosity, but we did our best by carrying out chores around her house, walking her sons to school and back home each day, and hunting down her pet dog each time it broke free of its shackles and escaped into the wilds of suburbia.

A ball hit across the backyard to the left of the pitch and over the boundary fence would land in the playground of the Kurdish preschool next door. Retrieving the ball from here required a team effort. Going through the front of the building and down to the back wasn't an option; the wrought-iron gates and solid brick walls that greeted you were impenetrable. The only way in was over the boundary fence, which was double our height. Two stacked milk crates provided some leverage, but the rest of the span needed to be made up with a two-person boost over the pinnacle of the fence. Some overzealous boosters would send my bony frame straight over the fence, and the only thing my hands or feet would touch, after what seemed like an eternity, was the ground when they came crashing down onto it. Once I'd retrieved the ball and thrown it back over the fence, the game would continue. Retrieving the retriever was of less priority than the ball and you had to spend some time being chased by a pair of grumpy geese before being pulled back to safety.

'Ya Ummoh!'

I was now outside the door of the granny flat at the end of the driveway.

'Ya Ummoh!' Mum finally called back from inside.

I opened the door and walked in to find her and Dad sitting down enjoying a plate of freshly cooked molokhia.

Dad used to grow molokhia in our backyard when we were younger. Harvesting it and then plucking its leaves off the stem, for cooking or drying for the wintertime, was an event that took place across many Arab households. Our backyard was a smorgasbord of Mediterranean fruits, vegetables and herbs. Both Mum and Dad had grown up on orchards in Lebanon and they made sure that their 600-square-metre block of Australian soil looked just like home.

Our house was occupied by nine children and two adults, eleven souls sharing one toilet in the early years. I was child number seven, way down the pecking order of lavatory privilege. When I'd dance around the house with a bursting bladder, Mum would send me off to relieve myself under the lemon tree behind the garage. I didn't know it at the time, but I was doing that tree a favour. Whenever Dad went into the toilet, I rained down urea onto the base of the lemon tree, and eventually its boughs were bent down to the ground under heavy fruit. It bore so much fruit that my brothers and I would use the lemons for throwing practice. The objective was to throw the lemon across as many backyards as possible. We rarely ever made it past more than one yard,and they'd almost always land in our cranky Serbian neighbour's garden. There'd always be a knock on our front door, not long after we'd launched our juicy projectiles, to complain about our antics. However, we continued to throw the lemons in her direction. This was not out of spite, but simply because there were no tall structures between our yard and hers, and throwing them in any other direction would almost certainly have meant breaking a glass window.

Mum and Dad invited me to sit down and have dinner with them. This was the only place I could enjoy molokhia so I couldn't refuse, not that Lebanese parents give you a choice when it comes to sharing a meal. We ate together and enjoyed some small talk before I announced my intention to depart. I gave both of them a hug and a kiss on the cheeks and forehead. Mum's hijab smelt like lavender fabric softener and spearmint-flavoured Extra gum.

I walked back up the driveway, past the point where I'd scraped my face across the wall the first time I rode a bike without training wheels, past the point where I'd planted my face into the concrete after jumping off a picket fence and broken my nose, and finally past the point where each of us nine siblings had departed on our wedding days.

Two days later Mum and Dad left the driveway. Only Dad returned.

TOTAL FIRE BAN DAY

CHER COAD

It's my mother's memorial day. The weather is hot, dry, windy – the whole world on the edge of burning. It's the summer of 1997 and I have just turned nineteen. The Victorian government has announced a day of total fire ban.

I have been shillyshallying all day, wondering if I should pay tribute to my mother as usual. In Chinese tradition, there are two days in the year when we can burn joss money, also known as ghost or spirit money, for our dead loved ones: the day of Qingming Festival and on their memorial day. Only on these days are they able to receive the money. The dead use the joss money to buy food and clothes and to pay the land master in their world. Mourning for the dead is also comfort for the living.

In Chinese culture, Yang Jian, the living world, is strongly associated with the sun, light and knowing, and includes all the things we can see and touch. At variance with this world, Yin Jian, the world of the dead, musters the forces of darkness, ignorance, the unknown and the afterlife. Yet the two worlds are actually not so different, or at least not so separate. Yin Jian is born from the world of the living, and the life that goes on after death is a continuation of the life preceding it. Thus death is neither an end nor a beginning.

I have lived in Melbourne for two years. I miss my family, especially my mother. Last night I had a dream. I was flying in the air like an angel. People were flying with me. Clouds were springing up around me, softly. I opened my arms to embrace the white clouds – I saw the sunset, flame-like, burning with golden stripes. Suddenly, people were disappearing and I started falling. I heard calling. I saw my mother. She was looking at me, her eyes full of longing and sadness. I shouted, 'Mum! Mum!' My mother flew to me. I reached out to her.

She looked pale. 'How did you get here?' I spoke in English with my Chinese accent. She stroked my hair without answering. At her gentle touch, my tears ran down. 'Oh, Mum, I've missed you.' I couldn't stop speaking in English. Don't speak English to her! Speak Chinese! I was fighting with myself in the dream. My mother saw my struggle, her eyes full of love.

'I missed you too,' she answered in Chinese.

'Do you understand English?' I was amazed.

'I understand you.' She smiled, with the smile that always warmed my heart.

'I thought you were dead …'

My mother embraced me with eyes as soft as the clouds. 'I have been with you all this time.'

Her words confused me. 'How? I am in Australia …'

'Distance doesn't concern me. When you think of me, I'll be with you.' She said this in her normal voice, so convincingly. Yet still I wasn't certain.

'Can you hug me, Mum?' I had been longing for my mother's hug ever since her death, longing for her physical body, which I could never embrace again.

To my surprise, she hugged me, and I felt the hug. My heart sang with satisfaction. 'Oh, Mum, it is really you. I thought I had lost you forever!'

'You will never lose me. I'll always be with you.'

The white clouds were suddenly extinguished. The sunset had turned the sky into gold. I held my mother and would not let her go.

'Promise me you will come to see me tomorrow.' My mother held me tightly, her hand stroking my hair.

'Of course, Mum.'

According to the old people, if the dead ones come into your dreams, it's time to send them joss money.

Living in Melbourne, I no longer have access to the Chinese agricultural calendar. Qingming Festival, also known as Tomb Sweeping Day, changes every year, in a similar way to the Easter dates, but even more complicated to calculate. While I was trying so hard to learn English, to learn Western culture, Qingming secretly passed me by. I had been longing for my mother's memorial day for months, worried that she would run out of money.

I wasn't able to look after her when she was alive. My only consolation now is looking after her in the other world. I believe there is an afterlife. In this way, she is still with me. I have promised I will never let her suffer again from a shortage of money and food, as when she was younger. This belief makes me feel at ease. Every time, after the joss-money ceremony, I have a sense of relief and contentment, which lasts for months.

I struggle to focus in language class, worrying about getting all the items for my ceremony. However, one topic of discussion catches my attention. The newly founded One Nation Party has started a cultural war towards new immigrants, especially Asians. In an article we are studying, Pauline Hanson says that new immigrants have brought their unwanted laws and culture to Australia. Some of my classmates have already been assaulted by young people, or had eggs thrown at them in the street. 'Go back to your own country!' people shout.

Most of my classmates are afraid. I am too.

After finishing language school, I rush to the Chinese grocery store and buy millions in joss money – also apples, bananas and oranges – for my mother's memorial day ceremony. I am excited. Also worried. Should I conduct the ceremony with Pauline Hanson all over the airwaves? And when the radio is constantly intoning: 'Today is a day of total fire ban'?

On the bus, I hold my treasures tightly to me. I worry the foreign objects in my bag will catch someone's attention. I see a middle-aged woman, a bit like Pauline Hanson, looking at me and my bag. I feel a sense of guilt and have disturbed speculations.

I call my Australian husband in Hong Kong to ask him about

my ceremony. He comes out of his meeting. He tells me that it's against the law.

'Maybe you can do the ceremony after the fire ban,' he suggests.

I start to feel desperate. 'But she will not receive anything if I miss today.'

'Darling, do it much later, when everyone's asleep, and make sure you don't start a fire.' He returns to his meeting.

While I am making my mother's favourite dumplings, time passes slowly. On the TV, Pauline Hanson is speaking passionately, with her unmistakable shortness of breath and high-pitched voice. She is demanding the parliament abolish multiculturalism. She says that Asians have swamped Australia and their culture will never assimilate into Australian culture. I am terrified. I feel she is addressing me directly. I turn off the TV, still questioning whether or not to perform the ceremony.

I decide to scout a safe location for it. According to Chinese tradition, the ceremony has to be conducted at an intersection, where it's easier to make the delivery to the other world. I live in Willington Crescent, East Melbourne. I spot the best place for the ceremony on the corner of Jolimont Road and Wellington Parade. A perfect place, concrete everywhere, with no possibility of causing an unwanted fire.

Meanwhile, my husband is calling me again and again. He has just had dinner at the Hong Kong Foreign Correspondents' Club. All the members are talking about is Pauline Hanson. He has also seen reports of some incidents of violence against Chinese people in Melbourne. He is terribly worried. 'Darling, you might not fully understand the situation due to your limited English.

Chinese people have been assaulted on the street in Melbourne. You should stay home for a while. I am coming back this weekend.' He is not supposed to come back for another two weeks.

I swirl on the floor like a child.

'I don't think you should do the ceremony tonight, it's too much of a risk. Especially when I am not with you. Please!' He is half pleading and half demanding.

'Okay, I won't do it.'

'Promise me.'

'I promise.'

I put the phone down. This is the second promise I have made that I know I will struggle to keep. Last night I made a promise to my mother. Now to my husband.

I can't sleep but I am too scared to turn on the TV. The uncooked dumplings are waiting on the table. I am wrestling with myself as if my pants are on fire. I can explain things later to my husband, but how can I explain to my mother when she so rarely comes into my dreams?

Eleven-thirty. The whole world asleep.

I gather up the joss money and colourful fruit. The fragrance of my plate of freshly cooked dumplings reminds me of my childhood with my mother. I nervously walk through a side gate to get to my chosen spot. The night is silent, still very hot, no wind. No cars. No people. Only my mother is waiting for me, somewhere, I say to myself.

I use a specially prepared stick to trace a circle on the ground, and place the plate of fruit next to the dumplings inside the circle. The circle distinguishes our world from the other world. The paper money will only burn within the circle, and the flames and smoke will only go up towards the sky, never leaving the circle.

I kneel on the ground. I feel a soft wind blow past me.

'What are you doing?' It's a man's voice, full of authority.

I look up. Two policemen, a tall one and a younger one, are standing there. My guilty conscience makes me feel cowardly. I don't know what to do. Another soft wind blows past me. I murmur, 'Mum ...' An unbearable loneliness and yearning strikes me, and tears silently rush down my cheek.

'Are you alright?'

'Can we help you?'

There is true concern in the policemen's voices.

Unconsciously, I put my finger to my mouth. 'Ssh, I am talking to my mother. I will explain to you after. Please.'

'That's fine. Go ahead. We are going nowhere.' The tall policeman speaks in a velvety voice. They move a couple of steps away, watching me.

I strike a match and set the joss money alight, choking with sobs. 'Mum, I am sending money to you, please come and collect it ...'

As I continue chanting in Chinese, the red flame brightens my heart, illuminating my soul. Slowly but surely I stop sobbing. The joss money continues to burn. Grey ashes are airily drifting in the circle that I have drawn, fluttering towards the sky.

When the last bit of fire burns out, the tall policeman breaks the spell out of sheer curiosity. 'What's this all about?'

'It was amazing.' The younger policeman sounds a note of relief for us all. 'Are you feeling better?'

I nod with boundless gratitude. 'Thank you so much. It's a ceremony for my mum.' I start tearing up again. Mum – the thought of her and the word 'mum' – is enough to break my heart. In a strange country, so far from my loved ones, only this ceremony has made me feel the everlasting loss of love.

'I'm sorry. I know it was a total fire ban day.' I am embarrassing with my vulnerability.

'It's okay. Lucky there isn't any damage. Otherwise we'd have had to handcuff you and take you to the station.' The younger policeman tries to light up the air once more.

I smile.

'What were you burning?' the tall policeman asks.

'Money.'

'Money!'

'Not real money. Money for my mum.'

'Where …?' the younger policeman begins to ask, before his colleague hushes him.

Again, a soft wind gently touches me. 'Can I have a hug?' I ask.

The St. Patrick's church bell strikes midnight and, with a hug, I leave behind the total fire ban day.

PINK RIBBONS

SAM PRICE

It was eighth grade when I was first called a dyke. I had my hair cut short and wore dirt smudged across my cheeks daily. This, teamed with my knickerbockers and softball glove, made me an easy dig. At the time, Google was my go-to for words too risky to ask Mum about, and so I went around the locker room boasting about how the boys at training said I was as tough as the walls that stopped floods. I was quickly corrected.

I stopped playing softball. And started ballet. I had thought it was cool and edgy to reject all things pink and pretty. After all, I'd built my whole personality on my inability to relate to other girls. Ballet wasn't serious or anything, I only did it for the exercise. But she liked it. So I found myself liking it too. She had this relentless, excitable energy, as if there were fireworks behind her eyes, waiting to erupt. She had glossy skin that bounced rays of sunlight across the room. Cheeks, soft and bouncy, like pillows begging to be fallen into. She had an admirable wit, cracking far too many jokes that I didn't understand but laughed way too hard at anyway. Sometimes she even wore a pink ribbon. I hated it.

We'd lie on the sportsfield before class, pretending we were testing hypotheticals, forcing jokes every time our eyes met. Testing the waters of friendship. Pitter patter. Pas de deux. We'd partner in the rain. Mud etched into our stockings. Raindrops resting atop her lashes. Grass stuck to her wet lips. If I stared too long she'd wipe it away. It was a hot December that year. She'd rest her head on my stomach as we splayed across the grass. Sweat dripping into our ballet buns, untangling them. Every giggle bounced the fly-aways atop her head.

'Girls,' Ms Kathy would call, clapping her hands with poise. We'd jump apart immediately and run up to class, as if we weren't doing anything wrong.

She offered to do my make-up for the end-of-year concert. We tucked ourselves away in the furthest corner of the dressing room. A crevice of free-standing wardrobes and music stands. We sat cross-legged facing each other, surrounded by palettes of pigments, false lashes and liquid glitters. My hands tightly gripped my knees. Uncharted waters. She dusted tiny brushes across my eyes, a delicate finger wrapped under my chin. Her breath, light, against my neck.

'Look up,' she whispered, tilting my chin gently. Her face inches from mine. A tiny line between her brows deepened with focus. 'Look up,' she giggled. I reluctantly lifted my chin, still staring down my nose at her. She rolled her eyes.

'Sorry,' I muttered, glancing up. The blandness of the ceiling was unbearable. She tapped a ring finger underneath my eye. Pressing product into my unslept skin. Her face blurry in my peripherals, but inches away.

She sat back, surveying her work. In what would have been a harmless gesture to those sure of their friendship but which was an eruption of chaos for me, she dropped her hand from my chin to my knee. And I imploded.

'What?' she snickered, my hyperventilation impossible to ignore. And as if to test my uneasiness, she put the brush down and rested her other hand on my leg. I held my breath. She unfurled each finger around me, holding my gaze, testing me. My fingernails cut into my palms. The quiet echo of classical music boomed through our secret corner. She lifted her hands from my thighs and before I could take a breath, wrapped them around my face, pressing her lips against mine. I could feel a bead of sweat run down the back of my leotard.

The door cracked loudly. We jerked apart. In the doorway another dancer froze, halted by shock, then disgust. Not a word was said, but the slam of the door confirmed my dread.

My red lipstick clung to her stone-white face, drained of colour. Her hands remained in the air, around a face withdrawn. The hesitation of youth and guilt lingering on her fingertips. She dropped them into her lap. Then picked up the make-up brush.

'Close,' she instructed, and I obeyed, latching my eyelids together.

I danced my worst that night, blaming my tears on the bright lights and future plans to miss 'these days'. I left early, and lay awake thinking. There were only two options: admit and accept my own repulsiveness, or blame her. Fears of ignored sleepover invitations and judging looks in the change room clouded my morality. I went to class on Monday with a sickening plan to protect my reputation. I spread a thick green fog of lies across the schoolyard. Whispers of obsession, assault and scandal synonymised with her name. World-class bullying, from the mouth of barely a teen.

As an adult, I try to blame my actions on immaturity and a bigoted childhood. But my brother prospers, with a better relationship with my family than ever since telling them the truth. So I really have no excuse.

—

It was tenth grade when we ended up in the same camp group together. And whether it was that two years feels like a lifetime ago at that age, or simply because there was so much left unsaid, we began talking again. It started with encouraging murmurs on particularly difficult trails, then snickering at dirty innuendos (which I now finally got), then progressed to whispers in the tent once the rest of the camp had fallen asleep. We couldn't keep our chuckles under our breath when our supervising teacher reprimanded the boys for sneaking into the girls' tents.

'Girls in the girls tents, and boys in the boys tents. I will have no funny business this week,' Miss Matthews scolded. I remember snorting loudly at the innocent expressions of the others.

The look Miss Matthews gave the two of us that day was the same look I've seen countless times since. From my GP, confused as to why I'm not concerned about pregnancy when I don't use birth control. My co-workers, when I rephrase their question from boyfriend to partner. I've even pictured that look on my own face, when questioning my sexual experiences. When does one lose their virginity if the rules of virginity don't include you?

—

It was twelfth grade when others began noticing her. And quickly I became second best to her boyfriend. It was fine. It wasn't like there was anything going on between us. At schoolies, we celebrated at a mutual friend's place. I drowned my jealousy in lost games of beer pong as the others compared red tongues after jello shots. Sometimes she and I would catch eyes, and I'd hold on just long enough for him to storm out. He'd blame some obvious lie and I'd sit on the staircase and braid her hair till he returned.

On the last night, he came back earlier than expected. Accusatory on arrival. Like he could smell the shared shower on us.

'I was drunk, baby,' she whimpered, clinging onto his shoulder.

'I thought you guys broke up,' I yelled.

But the incessant shaking of his head denied our pleas. A crowd shuffled around us. Circling us like sharks around prey.

'It wasn't my fault, baby,' she cried, 'she did it.'

She shook her index finger at me. 'She's a fucking dyke.'

I remember feeling my stomach churn. And the despicable smirk he gave. The room fell silent except for the unignorable bass of the EDM playing in the other room. She stopped crying almost immediately, like the faucet had been twisted off as soon as our unspoken promise was broken. I don't remember much else after that.

—

It was three years before we spoke again. I'm not sure who reached out to who. We both came up with excuses for our mistakes. Mine, immaturity; hers, drunkenness. We caught up for lunch and shared a bowl of wedges, unable to commit to the seriousness of a full meal. We danced around the topic for half an hour or so, before finally breaking it open. We managed to talk it all out. Got back on 'good terms', as they say.

I still hate pink ribbons.

But I love doing make-up. And I love going to the ballet.

When I go back to my home city for weekends, we bump into each other at shopping centres. We exchange pleasantries. Keep it casual. But I can't help wondering if I had the same impact on her that she had on me. Did I teach her about her sexuality? Did I help shape her identity?

Does she write short stories about me?

COEXIST

ROSIE OFORI WARD

Growing up I felt my life existed in two halves, that there were two distinct individuals living inside my body, two distinct cultures.

Some days I could see them, even feel them. I saw them fight. Felt them collide.

Watching from afar I shaped them, gave them form and even named them. I imagined Akosua's short dark hair and Mary's angular face.

The girls had their own lives, own childhoods, but somehow shared the same body, my body.

It was easier that way, to split my life in two.

Akosua was an angry child. My mum always said I had a tiger inside me, which would appear without warning, and I never did have the heart to tell her I had given that tiger a name. Akosua means 'born on a Sunday', a name one in seven girls in Ghana share. It is associated with the sun and thus with fire. A firecracker, that's what my teachers called me. A match about to suddenly ignite. Akosua would scream as a child. From her day-care in Westmead all the way down the M4, stopping only at the Nepean River. There was something about the water that subdued her. Put out her flame.

Mary on the other hand was contemplative, thoughtful. She shared her name with every second-born in my mum's family. Was always doing her best to fit in. She had this innate ability to mimic, to adjust. In the evenings she would arrange her impressive collection of multicoloured beanie bears on the end of her bed. She would imagine them as friends, disciples even, a whole kingdom to rule over. Mary was always good at imaginary games, they were the only places she was able to make the rules.

Akosua's home smelled of peanut soup and chilli. There were kente cloth curtains and wooden masks on every spare bit of wall. Her parents never did think to wonder if this had been a source of the night terrors that tormented her from ages four to nine. On the weekends at Ghanaian events with her family, Akosua would come alive. She made friends easily, tried to learn the dances and eat the spicy food despite Mary's complaints. She learnt to say Hello, Goodbye, How are you, I'm good and God bless you in Twi. It was Mary who learnt to say, I'm sorry I only speak English.

—

In the summers, Mary and her family went to the South Coast, always to the same house. There was one summer where she sang along to the same Delta Goodrem song for hours on end, until her sister threatened to snap the CD. One afternoon at the local

shopping centre her mum left her with the trolley as she popped
into the bakery. A woman, dripping in beige with pearls around her
neck, approached Akosua. She began to question her, demanding
to know where she was from, where had she got the piles of food
in the cart. Mary tried to explain that she and her family were
there on holiday from Sydney. But the woman was unconvinced
and before Akosua had time to step in, she was taken to security.
Her mum came to collect her, a package of soft white rolls under
her arm.

Are you sure she's yours?

Her mum scoffed and pulled her away, explaining, frustrated,
exhausted, that some people are just ignorant. In the back of the
car Mary inspected herself in the rear-view mirror. She looked
identical to her mum, didn't she? Same chin, same big eyes. But
she had forgotten that Akosua controlled the tone of her skin and
wide flat nose.

———

In class, Akosua gets into an argument with a boy. A cute boy, a
boy Mary has a crush on. He is explaining about people in other
countries, poor countries, people in Africa. They don't care as
much about their dead, it happens so much over there, he says.
They just throw away their dead and get on with their lives.
Akosua is yelling. She is talking about the funerals she has been
to, the night-long celebrations of life. The ceremonies that last
weeks in Ghana, about her dad letting her practice tying his thick
red and black funeral cloth. Later, as they are walking home, the
boy laughs, You get so angry in arguments. She stops beside him

as he ties his shoe and thinks about slapping him, thinks about grabbing him by the throat. She wonders if her tiny hands can fit around his neck.

A few weeks later Mary has agreed to go to the Year 10 formal with him. She has told him to buy a pink and white corsage to match her dress.

—

Chemicals on chemicals burn her scalp, straightening Mary's hair. There is a symphony of sound in the salon, a loud Afrobeats CD and the fast-paced unrelenting chatter of the hairdressers as they work. Akosua attempts to translate a sentence, even a single word. One of the women notices her inquisitive eyes and smiles. When her father appears to collect her, the woman chides him. How could you not teach her the language? He just sighs. It is the same story Akosua has heard a thousand times, excuses spouted to camouflage his fears. Why would she need it in Australia? Akosua wants to pipe up, explain the importance of culture, of talking and communicating with people like herself, but Mary is too busy admiring her new hair in the mirror. When she washes it later that week, the curls spring back. She begins to spend hours every morning with her straightener, begging it to remain flat. The next time Mary visits the salon, she asks them to leave the chemicals on longer. She puts in earplugs, tuning out the salon sounds, and grimaces as the chemicals burn.

—

Akosua decides she wants to write stories. Stories about people who look like her. About what it's like to feel out of place. She sets to work reading, Maya Angelou, Alice Walker, Toni Morrison, but is confused when these women's stories don't sound like hers. She writes a story and hands it to a teacher she admires. She watches him carefully as he reads the words, leaning back in his chair, crossing his arms. He shakes his head.

You're going to have to pick a new topic if you want to get good marks. He says there are no more black stories to tell, I mean all this suffering is a bit overplayed, isn't it? He laughs.

When Akosua leaves the room that afternoon, it is Mary who asks her friend to tell the teacher she is sick. Because Akosua couldn't say a man she admired had broken her heart that day, couldn't say she felt betrayed. Mary later hands in a story about a robot uprising and tops the class – much more accessible.

—

Mary sits alone in another room full of white students watching a video. She is doing a better job of blending in now. She has learnt to mimic their behaviour. If she speaks in slang and does her make-up just right, then maybe, just maybe, they won't see Akosua there beneath her skin. They are watching a documentary, *Race and Intelligence: Science's Last Taboo*. It discusses the science of why black people are less intelligent. There's an interview with a man who explains it all, he says Australian Aboriginals are the least intelligent race, with West Africans coming in a close second. Behind him sit accolades and degrees from important institutions, like the one whose application sits in her top drawer at home. A boy two seats to Mary's right yawns, he is playing candy crush on his phone. Later, when Akosua goes to speak to the teacher, she's told it's just the syllabus, they know it's a bit old-fashioned but what can you do. She cries herself to sleep that night.

—

I'm not sure if it's Mary or Akosua now. They're starting to blend into one, the edges of their worlds blurring beyond my control.

At first they fight it.

Mary seeks out white spaces, white hobbies, white men. A sense of safety, a sense of security. She tries to convince the world she belongs. She learns violin, goes to folk concerts, travels to England to visit family. She begins to talk like her mum, rounding her vowels.

Akosua lets her rage fuel her. She argues with her dad about not knowing the language, not knowing the culture. She starts a Twi language course online, cuts off her hair and throws out half her wardrobe, she can no longer even look at stripes.

At night I hear them, fighting in my head, whispering away.

Akosua's words are not her own, she's learnt them. Heard them yelled from car windows, spat across playgrounds and from the lips of those she loved, those she admired. This is not your country. This is not your home. You are not from here.

With Mary it's always the same refrain. The same mantra chanted under her breath. I belong here, I belong here, I belong here.

They lose friends, quietly, quickly, day after day. They tell Mary she never used to care about these things, never used to be so political. They tell Akosua she doesn't have enough rage, fire, enough understanding.

But the battle inside is nothing to what rages beyond. Nothing to the strangers, passers-by or even friends who tear at their skin. And as Mary bleeds, it is Akosua who ties the bandage. As Akosua cowers in fear, it is Mary who extends her hand. They feel it, each other's pain and dread, and seek solace and protection in each other's arms. They discover that to fight they must lean on each other, learn to get along. Or at least to coexist.

—

The weekend before they leave home, they lie on the beach under the Australian sun with their family and cannot help but smile as their melanin glows. They try to embrace all their parts, all their faults, all their mistakes and all their futures. They leave the familiarity of their town of one black family and move to a city where they learn to be one of many. They take with them one African mask and one orchid from their mum's greenhouse. The first night in their new home they watch Jane Austen and eat jollof rice. Compromise.

They don't fight quite so often now. Most days they blend so seamlessly, their thoughts overlap. I have begun to forget the cracks that used to loom so large. Black, white. Mixed-raced, biracial. British, Ghanaian, Australian. From Mpraeso, from Berkshire.

Coloniser, colonised.

Now, when I visit my parents in my childhood home, I see the memories of the two little girls who used to live there. They watch me still, out of mirrors and reflections in windowpanes. But now they're smiling.

As I explore my new world, I walk between those girls, Mary on my left, Akosua on my right. I feel safe there, I am the product of their two halves. Between them, I am whole. Between them, I belong.

INDEPENDENCE DAY

LAL PERERA

Two days after I became a ten-year-old, two days and thirty-five years after Ceylon became independent of British rule, I was sprinting between tut-tutting Aunties in the sweaty heat of the Noranda Community Centre kitchen when my shoulder caught the edge of a tray and I sent a huge stack of roti and two plates of kirributh crashing to the floor. I froze, mortified. Every Sri Lankan Aunty in Perth let out a howl of despair and I felt my breath actually stop. From somewhere within the crowd my mother emerged, her eyes bulging with rage. I'd never seen her so angry. But when she saw all the Aunties watching, she took a deep breath and said to me, very quietly: 'Outside. Now. Don't come back in here at all.'

I sat on the worn concrete steps at the back of the community centre, my stupid head in my stupid hands, the sun merciless at the back of my neck. I listened as someone made a speech welcoming everyone to the West Australian Sri Lankan Association's Independence Day Gala Lunch, as 'Sri Lanka Matha' played on a boom box, followed by 'Advance Australia Fair'. I heard Uncle Ranjith sing baila songs, and I heard everyone joining in on the choruses. I watched the cricket match start on the oval. I watched my cousin Mandy walk over towards me.

Controversial – scandalous – fourteen-year-old Mandy, whose schoolfriends (we'd heard) didn't even know her real name was Manjula, who (we'd heard) smoked cigarettes after school, who (we all saw) wore her hair and her skirts shorter than any other girl cousin; shorter, maybe, than any Sri Lankan girl in Perth.

She sat next to me, dropping her army-surplus bag between her feet.

'Hey, Twerp,' she said.

I looked up at her, then back to her bag, which I'd seen many times before at the bus station on the way to school: its checkerboard pattern along the straps; its RAF cloth badge; 'The Specials', 'The Selecter' and 'The Beat' handwritten in huge letters.

'Why did you bring your schoolbag?' I asked.

'It's not my schoolbag. It's my everything bag.' We looked out to where the cricket game had dissipated into drifting clusters of dads and kids. A group of teenagers sprawled in a surly circle at third man.

'You're the hot topic here today, Twerp. You know that?'

I looked up at her. 'What do you mean? What hot topic? Because I spilled the food?'

'What? Nah. Some nutjob thing you did with sandwiches.'

'What? Oh ...' I suddenly realised what she meant. 'Oh that? Geez!'

'Geez?' she laughed. 'You don't have to say "geez" with me! Say "Shit!" Say "Jesus!" Say "Jesus Fuck Shit!"' My eyebrows flew up with shock. I felt my whole scalp move and my glasses slide down my nose. She laughed again. 'What did you do? From what I'm hearing, it sounds like some seriously deranged shit.'

I told her.

Every Friday, my mother made fish curry sandwiches for us to take to school. The brown-red sauce, heady with garlic and karapincha, bled into the bread. One Friday afternoon, when everyone in Year 5 had wet hair and a huge appetite from swimming lessons, Josh Murphy and Dan O'Doherty spotted what I had in my lunchbox.

'Oh my god! What do you have for lunch, Lal?' shouted Murph. 'A shit sandwich?'

'That's disgusting!' laughed Dan.

'It's fish,' I meekly offered.

'That's not fish, mate. That's shit!'

I kept eating while everyone laughed. I didn't know what else to do.

The next Friday, I didn't take my lunchbox out of my bag. Murph and Dan moved on to fighting each other and my lunchtime problem evaporated. But that was lunchtime. Once I was home, I was in my bedroom with a fish curry sandwich and a house full of rubbish bins that my father emptied, rubbish bins whose contents couldn't be kept secret. I am not easily panicked now, and I was not easily panicked then: a calm, level-headed process of decision-making led to my secreting the sandwich on my bedroom bookshelf, behind the Narnia books.

And that's what I did every Friday.

My collection of sandwiches stretched past the Narnia series, of course; it colonised all the hidden spaces on all the shelves in my room, and, hidden as it was, as neat a solution as it was, I only thought about all that rotting bread and fish in the moments I was adding to its bulk. Fifteen seconds after I'd nudged in a new sandwich, I'd forget it and all its companions. Problem solved.

But two Saturdays before my birthday, when I was at Aunty Lalani's place, my mother decided to clean out my entire room, find the books and toys and clothes that could be given (back) to St Vincent de Paul and 'get rid of all the lata-pata'.

I returned home to find her on the back patio, reading her *Good News Bible* next to a small, black, stinking garbage bag.

'Thank you for looking after him, Lalani,' my mother said. 'But Lalith and I need to talk now.'

—

'Jesus Christ, you're gross,' said Mandy.

'I just forgot they were there.'

'Jesus, twerp. Your room must have smelled worse than it usually does. So what happened? Did you get spanked?'

'Yep.'

'Your mum or your dad?'

'Both. Mum when Aunty Lalani had left. Dad when he got home and she told him about it.'

'Ha. Double trouble.'

'And I had to go to confession after school the next Monday.'

'Did you confess it?'

'What happens in the confessional is a sacred secret,' I said, in complete earnestness.

'So you didn't confess it?'

I shook my head.

'Who here knows about it?' I asked.

'Everyone, as far as I can tell. You know how these things happen. Your mum tells five other mums while they're serving up the food and next thing you know it's the news of the day.'

'The hot topic,' I mumbled. I took off my glasses and wiped away tears with the back of my hand.

Mandy unleashed a long, rasping groan. I could hear her eyes rolling.

'Hey,' she said, 'look at this.' She lifted the bag onto her lap and I watched her unzip it enough to push her hand inside. When she drew it out again, her fingers were coiled around the neck of a bottle of 100 Pipers Scotch. 'You know what this is, right?'

'Yeah.'

'Of course. What would a family party be without Charles Seeya ploughing through one of these and thinking we don't notice?'

'Is it his?'

'No, you idiot. It's mine. It's how I make days like this tolerable.'

I didn't know what to say.

'And do you know what else?' Mandy said. 'I bought it with money I took from my mum's purse.'

'What? Really?'

'And you know how I didn't go to Achchi's birthday in December?'

'You had a debating competition.'

'Debating? I had a huge party to go to. It was massive.'

I still didn't know what to say, and she knew it, I could tell. She looked me straight in the eye. 'Are you going to tell on me, Twerp?'

'No. I wouldn't do that.'

'I know you wouldn't. You're learning, Lal. You're a good learner. Do you know what you're learning?'

'No.'

'You're learning that you have to lie. I'm not saying that it's okay to lie. I'm saying I know that sometimes lying is the best option. Do you understand?'

'Maybe. I'm not sure.'

'Lal, kids like us, people like us, we have to lie every now and then. There's no point in even telling my parents there's a party on with girls and boys – Australian boys, you know, white boys – so I have to lie if I want to go. And there's no point in telling my friends that I had to lie to get there, so I have to lie to my friends. Do you want to get into a fight with these dickheads in school and explain to them how the sandwiches you eat are the result of the Portuguese coming to where your ancestors lived and introducing chilli to their local food, and then all of that becoming the complex and delicious lunch you bring to school while they're wrapping their mouths around ham and mayonnaise?'

'I don't even like fish curry sandwiches, Mandy.'

'God! That's not the point! Do you like fighting to get to eat your lunch?'

'No.'

'No.' Mandy sighed again. She reached into the bag, pulled out the bottle and, in a flash, swigged some Scotch. 'What you have to do, Lal, is lie to Aussies about how Lankan you are and you have to lie to Lankans about how Aussie you are.'

'I have to lie?'

'Sometimes you do.'

'Oh.'

'But you need someone that you never lie to. That's going to be me. Okay?'

'Okay.'

'I mean it. Don't lie to me.'

'I won't.'

'And don't lie to yourself. That will fuck you up.'

'Lie to myself?'

'Lying to yourself. You'll know it when you do it. And when you know it, don't do it again.'

'Okay.'

'You don't like fish curry sandwiches?'

'I hate them.'

'Okay, then. I've got an out for you.'

'What's an "out"?'

'An out is an out. Don't lie to me, though. Okay?'

'Okay.'

'Never?'

'Okay.'

'And when you catch yourself lying to yourself, you'll stop it straightaway?'

'Okay.'

'Lie to the rest of these dickheads, though. If you have to.'

'If I have to.'

'If you have to.'

'Only if I have to.'

'Okay. Well, I have an out for you.'

For the next three years, Mandy would meet me at the bus station on Friday mornings. I'd hand over my fish curry sandwich and she'd hand over something else for me to eat. As she got older – as I got older – my Friday lunches became more elaborate and exciting. I don't know what it took for her to make that extra lunch every Friday, or what she did with my fish curry sandwiches, I don't know what lies she had to concoct to make that happen, week after week.

Mandy found an out for me and I loved her for it. I love her still.

WHEN ALIENS ATTACK

MONIKKA ELIAH

'She's an alien!' Timmy, a freckle-face with a bleached mullet, yelled out to my Year 2 class. I sat still while he took a fluoro-green bendy ruler out of his Hot Wheels pencil case and reached over the group table to measure the bare skin from my hairline to the top of my eyebrows. 'Yep! Definitely an alien.' He scribbled the exact centimetres down in his spelling book and wiped the ruler on his school shorts.

By his tone I knew he was insulting me, but I didn't know what the word meant. I didn't want to see him continue to study my head, so I trained my eyes on the blackboard, pretending I knew how to read the English words scrawled in a list.

Jessie, Jesse and Jessy, three girls who had once left half a tuna sandwich in the space under my school desk, giggled and hid their sharp yellow teeth behind pink hands. I hadn't seen the sandwich until the bread was as hard as a biscuit and the tuna looked like snot. Mrs Brown had been livid.

'I don't know what you did back home in Iraq, but here we do not hide food in our desks!' As punishment for being 'absolutely disgusting' she had made me sit in the corner of our classroom while everyone else made dot paintings of kangaroos using cotton buds and red and yellow acrylic paint. As I sat there, Jessie, Jesse and Jessy walked over to refill their paint cups and bragged about how it was them. Thinking of it now made my stomach squirm like I had eaten the snotty tuna myself.

When my other classmates started to whisper, I felt my ears begin to pulse and pushed the tip of my tongue to the roof of my mouth to stop my lips from trembling. I'm an alien. What is an alien? I tried to think of similar-sounding words. All in? Ant liar? I repeated 'alien' over and over in my mind, trying to trigger a memory. Was it on last week's spelling list? Maybe it meant stupid or ugly. Would I get in trouble for being an alien? Would they kick me out of school for being an alien? Was I the only alien or were there others in the class?

'Hands on heads!' Mrs Brown shouted, interrupting my thoughts, her face thrusting forward with enough force to jangle the carved wooden parrots hanging from her long lobes. The laughter stopped and twenty-five sets of arms shot up in the air and folded across heads. I tried to keep my elbows in line with my shoulders, resisting the urge to slouch into my plastic chair. I watched Mrs Brown's earrings continue to swing back and forth as my biceps started to tingle. I looked around the class and began to make a mental list. I was an alien. Timmy, Jessie, Jesse and Jessy were not aliens. Mrs Brown was not an alien. Not-Aliens had freckles, yoghurt skin, pink hands and yellow teeth.

'Hands down!' Mrs Brown instructed and gave us a moment to settle. I waited for her to say something but she didn't even look at me. I knew I had to find out whatever it was that made me an alien and fix it.

Since I was too embarrassed to ask any of my other classmates, I decided to wait until recess to ask Hallie. Hallie was the first Australian friend I had made since our arrival a few months prior. She lived next door to my family in a fibro house scratched up by the dozens of cats that slept in her front yard. She was very smart and had taught me important Australian customs, such as spitting on the floor before entering one's house and smearing wet hands on a bathroom wall to dry them. She had even once made me a special Australian food called 'fish sticks' which consisted of uncooked spaghetti noodles dipped in Vegemite. When I approached her, I felt my palms start to sweat. I knew Timmy was mean, so him saying I was an alien could be a lie, but Hallie was my friend. If she confirmed it, I would know it was true. I had to practice the sentence in my head beforehand so I could get the right English words out.

'Hallie, I am … am I an alien?'

She stared at me, twirling a strand of oily orange hair between her blue glitter nails. 'Yes,' she answered, nodding so that her fringe spilled over into her eyes.

I felt my heart clench and again I pushed the tip of my tongue to the roof of my mouth. I took a deep breath and asked, 'Hallie, what is an alien?'

Again she stared at me, continuing to twirl the strand of hair. 'I'll only tell you if you buy me a lime-flavoured fruit tube from the canteen.'

I didn't have money. I never had money. It was impossible for Mama to spare coins from an empty wallet. The one time I had asked she told me, 'When we can buy meat, you can buy snacks.' Afraid to turn down Hallie's offer, I nodded in agreement and began walking towards the canteen. Maybe I'd find some coins along the way. Maybe someone had dropped a coin in the bark chips below the nesting magpies. The nest was balanced in a tall tree that hung over the paved path to the canteen. Protecting their eggs, the magpies would swoop down to peck and scratch at students passing by. In the rush to evade the birds, students often dropped their money in this area. Peter Tran had once lost a fiver and had come to class with deep, bloody marks on his shaved scalp where the birds had attacked him.

As I approached the treasure pit, I ducked down and crab-walked over to avoid the magpies' claws and beaks, keeping my feet as flat as possible so creases did not form in the tops of my polished faux-leather shoes. I squatted by the tree roots, careful not to dirty my school dress, and began sifting through the red wood chips, searching for loose change. The first coin I found was five cents. That wasn't enough for a fruit tube. I kept looking, raking my hands across the dirt until I spotted another flash of silver. I dug, my fingernails getting filthy with mud, and pulled out a metal hexagon. Fifty cents! Grey and grimy, it was enough to get a fruit tube! Looking around to make sure no-one could see, I jumped up to run but stopped when a magpie turned its head my way. I waited for a scratch. Surely the bird would punish me for stealing from the pit. Desperate to be spared, I tried my hand at bargaining. 'If you let me go, I'll get you a breadstick!' The bird didn't respond but it didn't shift to attack either. I wasn't keen to test my luck so I backed my way out of the pit and then turned to walk once more along the path.

In the canteen line, I rubbed my knuckles across the metal coins, trying to clean the dirt caked on their surface. Would the canteen ladies know this wasn't my money? Would they call the police? I imagined a pencil-thin man in a navy suit coming to my classroom and telling me I had to be sent back to Iraq. Would I leave by myself or would they send my parents with me? It would be my fault. I was an alien and a thief. What would Australians do to an alien thief in prison? By the time it was my turn to buy, I had pressed the six edges of the fifty-cent coin so far into my sweaty palm I had branded myself with the Queen's face and crown.

'What can I get you?' the canteen lady asked between popping her gum.

'Lime fruit tube, please. One breadstick, please.' My hand was shaking when I handed over the money, the coins slipped through my fingers and fell, ringing out as they skipped across the countertop. The canteen lady glared at me and then put the coins into her apron pocket. She kept her eyes on me as she pulled a fluoro-green fruit tube from the freezer and snipped it across the top. She kept her eyes on me as she shoved her thick fingers into a biscuit tin to pull out a breadstick. She didn't hand my purchased items to me immediately. Just kept narrowing her eyes at my face until I couldn't see any part of them except for her mascaraed lashes. She knew. Whatever Timmy had seen on my face she could see too. She handed the two items to me and I took them with a quiet thank you. Running back down the paved path, I came to the magpies' nest and crumbled the breadstick down by the tree roots, the sesame seeds sprinkling across the loose leaves and bark chips. I waited for my punishment, but again, the magpies didn't move.

I was out of breath when I handed the fruit tube to Hallie. She took it quickly, as if she was afraid I would go back on our deal.

'Hallie, what is an alien?'

She took a long slurp, draining the ice of its colour. Her cheeks caving in, her nostrils flaring. When she began to speak, her tongue was stained garbage-bin green. 'An alien is a bad person. Like a criminal. They don't look like us. They fly around in a big spaceship like the airplane your family came in and they want to eat people's brains.'

'But I don't want to eat brains.'

'That's because you're a kid. Kid aliens eat regular-people food, but adult aliens eat brains.'

'Hallie, are you an alien?'

'No. Australians can't be aliens but we're very good at spotting them.'

The bell rang and I walked to line up outside my classroom. I was an alien and I would grow up to eat brains. I stared at Mrs Brown and tried to imagine eating her brain. Yuck! I'd rather eat magpie poop. In class, I repeated Hallie's words to myself. Not-Aliens had freckles, yoghurt skin, pink hands and yellow teeth. Whatever Timmy had first spotted was on my forehead. I noticed Not-Aliens like Hallie also had fringes.

After class, Mama was at the gate waiting for me. Her dye-box highlights shimmered in the sunlight and her perfume smelled like freshly cut cucumbers. On our walk home, in the linguistic switch from English to Assyrian, I felt anger replace my embarrassment. Digging my nails into my palms, I told Mama about how Timmy had laughed and called me an alien. She didn't know what the word meant either. When we got home we spent an hour staring at my forehead in the small magnifying mirror Mama used when she was threading the hairs above her eyes, trying to see what Timmy had seen.

'My forehead is big,' I announced, and in my frustration began to pull hair forward to cover it.

Mama reminded me that a big forehead meant a big brain, but I didn't care. I decided I wanted a fringe, like Hallie. I begged and whined until Mama threatened to leave me on the kerb for council collection. Finally, she caved and brought out the biscuit tin my father used to store sewing supplies. She pulled out a giant pair of metal scissors and used her fingers to comb forward a section of hair. After a deep breath, I heard her make the first snip. A few minutes later, looking back into the magnifying mirror, I was staring at a fringe that was shorter on the left than the right. I dug my hand around in the biscuit tin, searching for the black Texta my father used to mark the hem of his pants. Using it, I drew tiny dots across my nose and cheeks. My mother laughed and squeezed my hand. Her fingers were so warm that it was hard to believe she could eat human brains. I wanted to ask her but I was too scared to hear the answer. What if she said yes?

AN AUSSIE BBQ

SERPIL SENELMIS

Mambo was licking at my feet. It was forty-two degrees and the puppy wanted some of my pine-lime Splice, which was quickly melting into a gluey puddle. Mum said I didn't have to go to Turkish school today. Oh, happy days! I leapt up, unlocked my sticky fingers and grabbed my boogie board. 'Mum, can I go to Mullaloo Beach?' I asked excitedly. One of the girls at school had told me that the two hottest Year 9 boys were going to be there. I could just sit on the hot white sand and watch them surf all day. That would be the best Saturday.

Mum reminded me today was Kurban Bayrami, also known as the feast of the sacrifice. I was ordered to wear my finest summer dress and be ready within half an hour, as we'd be visiting friends. I protested that house visits were a stupid idea on such a hot day. Why couldn't they just meet us at the beach? Like. Normal. People. Mum shot back a deathly glare and screeched at me like a galah. I think I may have felt my internal organs twinge with fear.

Within an hour, my two sisters and I were all lined up across the scorching vinyl seats of the canary-yellow Toyota Corolla. I was the middle child but, at fourteen years old, I had the household reputation for being the bossiest and the most stubborn sibling. Mum used to say that if I was an animal I'd be a mule.

As the hot summer air blew in Dad's window en route to our destination, Mum gave us the usual speech: we were not to ask our hosts for anything, especially treats, we dare not complain about wanting to go home, and we'd better not be rowdy. Our parents wanted us to be model guests, otherwise we could bring shame on the family.

As we pulled out of our sprawling new residential development, which had more vacant land than homes, my sisters and I joked that we were off to the badlands. Our destination – Koondoola. Just fifteen minutes from the city, it had a reputation for being the epicentre of crime. Still, the residents, who were an assortment of newly arrived migrants, first-generation Aussies and Aboriginal Australians, happily got on with their lives. The neighbourhood had a lot of dishevelled commission houses, and that's where we were directly headed. I had packed my favourite Roald Dahl book, just in case I got bored.

When we arrived, we peeled ourselves out of the steamy car and spilled onto the burning pavement. We were greeted with double kisses and icy cold ayran, a salty yogurt drink. But before too long, I was singled out and bundled back into Dad's mate's car. We set off on another journey – this time to pick up a 'special package'. I was hoping it involved chocolate.

We headed towards Kalamunda, about thirty minutes away. Snaking our way up the hill, we saw orchards start to appear. Apricots, nectarines, plums. It was nature's supermarket. I got familiar flashes of signposts and guessed that we might be about to visit Mum's old boss. I just knew him as Tony, the kind Italian man who showered us with wheels of fancy cheese. If it wasn't for him, we'd just be eating generic Black & Gold.

But sadly, we weren't off to visit signor cheesemonger. We pulled into a primitive gravel driveway and I spent the next ten minutes feeling like I'd been thrust into an old tumble dryer. Finally, the engine stopped, and an old man ushered us onto his farm.

Dad's mate told me to pick out a lamb. 'Choose the one you love the most,' he bellowed. I pointed at a pair of innocent eyes. Then I was quickly whisked away by the old farmer's wife, who told me to pick some fresh nectarines and use my dress skirt to carry them. I attempted to carry my body weight worth of summer fruit back to the car. Needless to say, I loved a challenge.

After a while I could see Dad gesturing from afar. He said we were ready to head back. On our way, the car started coughing and clacking. At one point it sounded like a baby crying. Distressed, I asked what the weepy noises were. Dad's mate said the lamb was probably just a bit hot in the boot.

I yelped, 'The lamb's back there?'

He just chuckled and said, 'She's tough. She'll be alright.'

I could feel my shoulders tensing, and my cheeks were wet with tears.

What happened next was something I knew would be burnt into my skull for the rest of my days. We pulled up in Koondoola, popped open the boot, and the lamb tried to fling itself towards freedom. Blindfolded and with its legs bound, it was taken thrashing into the garage.

'You picked well,' Dad's mate said to me. He then whispered, 'Bismillah al-Rahman al-Rahim,' into the lamb's ear, pulled out his blade and painted the concrete red. The blood poured out of the tiny body like a faucet that had been turned on, until it reduced to a drip and turned into a colourful crust from the heat.

By now hordes of other guests had arrived. An army of women were making salads, rolling and frying dough, cooking pilavs, and making a selection of dips. Others were already preparing the desserts, from baklava and irmik helvası to chocolate mosaic cake (mozaik pasta) and sütlaç, a traditional rice pudding. The men were firing up the barbecue.

The host's son came outside. He wanted to know if I wanted to have a go on his new Nintendo Super Mario Bros. game. It was the one game every kid at the time wanted to play. But I couldn't pick up the console. I was too busy questioning whether I'd just helped murder a lamb.

After Dad's mate had disrobed the lamb, another one of the men picked up what was left of the lifeless body, put a hook in it and hung it up on a pillar. As he did this, I noticed the scars under his armpits. His skin had folds of unnatural creases. It looked like it would be painful. Without hesitating I blurted out, 'What happened to you?'

He had gentle but piercing eyes. He stopped what he was

doing, looked directly at me and said, 'It's a souvenir from my torturers.'

I wasn't sure what that meant, so I asked another probing question. 'Who tortured you and why?'

Dad told me to hush. But the forty-something-year-old wanted to unburden himself. He pointed at the lamb hanging feebly. He said, 'They hung me just like that and called it an Afghan hanging.' They had chained him to the ceiling of his cell and suspended him by his wrists for days. When he didn't tell them what they wanted to hear, they brought in the boiled eggs and pressed them into his armpits. His scars were the result of third-degree burns and days of horrific torture. His crime was speaking out against the government.

I'd helped open a chasm of old wounds and the conversation took on a sudden political agenda. The men immediately started debating the current state of governance back home, and before long nostalgia kicked in. They all took turns reminiscing about the dark days of 1980, when the military junta overthrew the forty-third government of Turkey. One of the men sighed and pulled out a can of beer from the esky he was sitting on. When he cracked it open and took a swig, another man took offence and said, 'This is a holy day.' The beer guzzler simply replied, 'God knows I have a pure heart', and kept drinking.

The women tried to lighten the mood. They summoned a ghetto-blaster, rewound the tape, and soon after folk-dancing music could be heard blasting out of the speakers. It was so loud, it echoed down the street. I wondered what the neighbours thought of all this racket. Forming a human chain, the women started the familiar Halay dance. It was like communing with our ancestors – from the other side of the world. The moves harked back all the way to our Anatolian pagan descendants, and even earlier than that, to the days of the Assyrian Empire, now only existing in history books.

As heart rates roused to the beat of the music, the smell of the freshly cooked lamb filled our nostrils and ayran continued to be splashed about. The game-happy young boy ducked his head through the flyscreen. 'You bored yet? I'm ready to kick your arse with Mario,' he grinned.

I put my game face on and replied, 'Oh, it's on!' and left the adults to try to solve the problems of today and days gone by.

FIRST TIME FOR EVERYTHING

MARGARITA D'HEUREUX

Two mince pies, please, Miss Lady.

I salivated and swallowed hard. The small cake shop in Strathfield was festooned with brightly coloured tinsel in hues of red and green. In the background, Bing Crosby crooned 'I'm dreaming of a White Christmas'. Tiny Santas sat atop iced Christmas cakes. On top of the counter were various sizes of gingerbread houses heavily decorated with icing, and snowmen made of marzipan stood guard at the front door. The roofs were decorated with colourful sweeties and soft jub jubs. Lollies, I reminded myself and not jub jubs … Jubes!

Reminder to self: don't ask for a zaboca – it's an avocado now. Don't look for chicken feet in the supermarket to make soup, you won't be able to buy them, and if you get a yearning for pig-foot souse, seasoned with chillies, lime, chadon beni and cucumber and eaten to celebrate Old Years' Night – or New Year's Eve as they say here – well, forget it, for the next decade or so!

Don't drop your verbs – like – 'ah gone dong de road'. Verbs are important in the English language, and don't ever steupsed! – that is, suck your teeth when you are annoyed. If someone asks if you are from Wales or England, nod enthusiastically. It can get complicated if they have not heard of Trinidad, unless they are cricket buffs. If they insist, tell them it's the most southern island of the Caribbean – close to Venezuela. If they look at you in a quizzical way – it's okay. Just smile and say proudly that your mother is of English heritage and your father is French. Within moments, you will be deemed exotic and interesting. The trick is to speak slowly and try acting like you are from the US or England – to avoid any unnecessary questioning, of course. But, Most Importantly, don't ever, ever end every single sentence with 'YEAH MAN'.

I stepped out of the cake shop into the heat of the midday sun. The sky was painted a flat blue with not a single cloud in sight. In the distance, cicadas hummed. I was looking forward to the mince pies. They were small and round and covered in a pale pastry, lightly dusted with icing sugar. Strange, I thought. I was in Australia now. Far away from the little dot in the Atlantic. Trinidad, West Indies. I took a bite ... but ... eh ... eh, what is dis ting? Oh gorsh, is too sweet, and it has sultanas and mixed peel with some kind of syrupy, sickly sweet gravy. Oh man! – but where is de mincemeat? It was Christmas, 1974.

The cicadas' faint hum was now a crescendo as I approached our rented home in Strathfield.

I found my father in the front yard. A hose in his hand spraying water into the trees.

Pa – yuh okay?

Nah man – these blasted cicadas too noisy! They worse than de steel-bands back home!

With that there was a sudden silence, but with the wave of a conductor, they seemed to break into an even higher crescendo. There was a long steupsed and my father turned the nozzle to a hard spout and continued to spray the trees. A determined look was etched on his face. I hurried inside, too embarrassed to stay any longer. I could see the elderly lady next door craning her neck over the fence, gazing at my father. She looked perplexed.

The house sat on a large block. I guessed a keen gardener once lived here. In the winter months, the garden beds were crammed with dainty snowbells, stunning sapphire blue anemones, and a profusion of Spanish bells that sat under the deciduous trees. Sunny daffodils poked their heads out in unexpected places. Camellias, heavy with flowers, stooped like old ladies, a spreading carpet of scarlet petals concealing the lawn beneath. Crowds of multicoloured azaleas under ancient gums basked. It was in this garden where my love affair with flowers and bulbs began, and the appreciation of the changing seasons.

I entered the large kitchen and found my mother and sister at the kitchen table. Hey Ma – what you doing?

Making pastelles, chile.

My mother had fine features, with fair skin, a sharp nose and pure blue eyes. Her cheeks were flushed pink from the heat of the kitchen.

But we don't have banana leaves to wrap the pastelles? All yuh using foil? I cried out.

I went to Franklins dis mornin to buy leaves, my mother said, and de people did not understand me. Den de man informed me Madam yuh need to go to Queensland to get dat.

I grimaced and said a silent prayer that I had not been there. My mother was 'vex'. In a more colloquial vernacular, she was cranky.

On the table there was an assortment of bowls filled with sliced boiled eggs, salty capers, plump sultanas and spicy minced meat. Under a damp tea towel were rows of cornmeal rolled into balls. My mother took one out, dipped it into oil and pressed it firmly with her fingers onto the foil, shaping it into a circle. Shirley, my older sister, placed the fillings on the cornmeal and then folded it over to hold the ingredients inside. Her hair, like my mother's, was short and sandy in colour but, courtesy of a home perm, tight curls hugged her head. There was much brushing to soften the recalcitrant waves, but with the humidity of summer they had a life of their own. Shirley secured the pastelles with string and placed them on the large pile at the end of the table. Later they would be boiled for twenty minutes in a large pot of water.

Later that afternoon, to escape the stifling heat of the house, I went into the backyard. The quietude of the cooler garden was now gone, replaced with a dry lawn, bare in patches. The camellias sat upright, devoid of their winter burdens. The bulbs had burrowed deep into the warm earth and patiently waited for the first sign of frost. Roses, as old as the house, with their gnarled trunks, sat in long beds. Large blooms hung their heads, sweet and aromatic; hungry bees swarmed.

I found my father in the front garden. He was asleep under the maple tree. Battle-weary from the day. Hair damp from perspiration. The hose was neatly wrapped, ready for tomorrow's gallant fight. For now, the cicadas had retreated, resting their timbal muscles and planning another attack for the hot day ahead. By now, grey clouds had rolled in, hugging each other against a dark sky. A cool change had sprung up. It caressed my warm face and tugged at my wiry curls. Large drops of rain began to fall. Plop … Plop. The parched earth sucked greedily. Far in the distance, thunder groaned. I heard my mother call.

Come and get dinner, de pastelles ready.

In a few days, on Christmas morning, we ate pastelles and smothered them in piccalilli. It tasted just the same as it always did. There was always a first time for everything.

CHECKPOINT CHARLIE

MAHA SIDAOUI

The Entertainment Guide (EG) was a supplement that came out in *The Age* newspaper every Friday. We circled the bands and the clubs that we wanted to go to but would never be allowed to. Having to be home at ten sharp made nights out impossible. Nothing worth listening to ever started before we were due back home in bed and the only person allowed out past this time was my brother, Omar.

The EG ran a competition asking readers to send in entries explaining why they liked clubbing. The prize was a hundred-dollar voucher to be spent at Checkpoint Charlie.

This club had just opened and we were all desperate to go. 'We' being me, my sister, Helda, and my girlfriend Sasha, who I went to school with. Sasha's parents didn't care what time she came home, and she was allowed out everywhere. We considered her one of the luckiest people in the world.

The day after the EG advertised the competition, we went to Sasha's house in Heidelberg and spent the day penning our masterpiece. Sasha's father, an American-history professor, would walk past the study and observe us from the doorway, shaking his head, more bemused than disapproving. We lay on the floor for hours, laughing, screaming, writing, laughing, screaming, writing. We even came up with a collaborative writers' name – The Heidelberg Hedonists.

The EG sent us the voucher and printed our winning poem.

A Slave to fashion.
Clothes are my passion
I'm into 'Rare Groove.'
Hair slicked back,
Clothes all black,
I think I'm real smooth.
Bank teller by light,
Clubber by night,
Decked out in my Najee.
Knocked back every time
Who knows? This rhyme,
Might get me into Checkpoint Charlie.

We were of course wannabe clubbers, writing about ourselves. My sisters and I were Lebanese. Lebanese Muslim girls trying to make sense of Australia through the pubs and clubs and all the cool people who went there. Najee, a fashion label owned by a Lebanese–Australian, was worn by everyone in Australia – except Anglo-Aussies. Najee had late-night ads squeezed in-between Erich Planinsek furs and never-ending sales for Franco Cozzo furniture, making sure us wogs knew where to shop to look sharp.

As wogs, my parents and their friends approved of a social life for their children that seemed inane to me. On weekends they let us go to Lygon Street. This involved getting dressed up in clothes fit for a wedding: heels, taffeta dresses and full faces of make-up. We walked up Lygon Street, then sat at Cafe Notturno, or 'Notts' for short. We ordered cappuccinos and I tried to puff away at my St Moritz menthol cigarette. While we chatted, boys checked us out and my older cousins repetitively told me, 'Don't look! Don't stare. Don't look. Don't look. Don't look! I said don't stare.' And even though I was never sure where to look and who not to stare at, boys still came over and talked to us.

We got to know some of the boys: Claude, Dominic, Maurice, Vince and Robert. They dressed in suit jackets with their sleeves rolled up to their elbows to reveal white shirts and chunky watches that dangled on their wrists. They wore Kouros aftershave, which I inhaled while we entertained each other with stories of our daily lives, imitating parents, friends and often each other. Humour was our self-defence: if we had been laughed at by others during the week, we came together to laugh at ourselves.

I felt superior if the boys singled me out to speak to me alone. I didn't care what they looked like or how uninteresting they were, I was desperate for them all to ask me out. I wanted them to take me somewhere, to put their arms around me.

The boys could all joke with me, pay me compliments and scan the room all at the same time. At first I thought they were worried their parents would walk in. Then I believed it was because they were embarrassed to be seen talking to me. I couldn't retain their full attention and began to question how I looked.

Even among all my cousins at Notts I still looked out of place. I had a Grace Jones haircut, inspired by my idol and cut by an intimidating hairdresser called Harry, who displayed an old black Chevy in the window of his Greville Street salon. I wore the approved black jackets and pants but I could never find high heels to fit my big wide feet, so I often 'borrowed' my brother's boots. Helda wore ever-so-tight skirts, pointy shoes, lace stockings and badges across the lapels of her jackets. While she flicked her electric-blue fringe and twirled her nose ring, the girls at Notts stared on and adjusted their shoulder pads. It was clear we didn't fit into the coffee scene that my parents approved of. There had to be something else out there for us. Of course there was. Checkpoint Charlie was just the beginning.

We had a month to use the voucher, but my sister decided that we would go the following Thursday. It was, according to her, 'the night all the cool people went out'. The majority of our discussions centred on our parents letting us go. We decided the perfect time to ask would be that Thursday at five-thirty pm. We didn't want them to have too much time to come to a decision. And we agreed that Helda would do all the talking.

We showed our parents the voucher and Helda explained that it was a fancy new restaurant. Dad took the rectangular steel-grey card, but it was the red star that caught his eye and held his attention. He read out the words 'Checkpoint Charlie'.

I sat on the couch next to Mum, and Helda balanced on the arm of her chair. Dad sat in his tan-coloured Moran recliner, his feet propped on the extended footstool, and considered the words with a large degree of concentration. Then, as he sat straight, the chair snapped out of recliner position. With a hint of pride, he announced, 'So the owner is a communist?' Answering his own question, Dad began to nod. We were in with a chance.

'Obviously, Dad.' Helda was calm and measured.

'The poem you wrote, let me see it.'

I wasn't expecting this.

'Sure, I'll go get it.' Helda did not move. Instead she tilted her head ever so slightly and said, 'You know, Dad, I think you'd like it. It's about a utopian society in which we all embrace this period of revolutionary transformation.'

My father nodded, liking what he heard. 'Do you know the owner's name?'

Helda went for gold. 'I don't know his name, but I hear he's a big supporter of Fidel.'

'Hmm, Castro. I believe he must be a good man.' My father waved his pipe around, which always meant a speech was about to follow.

Mum laughed and quickly covered it up with a cough. She often did this when my father talked politics. I didn't dare to look at her. Dad would get upset, yell at Mum, and then they'd scream the night away, mostly in Arabic.

'Castro is one of the great men, but still we have to think of Che Guevara. He believed in the good of society and …'

Mum grabbed my hand and shifted towards me in an attempt to hide her laughter.

Dad emptied his pipe into the orange-coloured glass ashtray. He stopped talking, lost in his thoughts, and said, 'You can go.' My heart raced, I wanted to scream, but judging by Helda's cool response I knew it wasn't in the bag – just yet. I stayed seated.

Then he opened a small wooden bucket filled with fresh-smelling tobacco already shredded and mulled, and packed his pipe. We all watched him, waiting. Leaning back in his chair he said, 'I want you to prepare a speech.'

Helda and I quickly shared a glance: we could be here for hours.

'They may ask you to say something after the dinner. Tell them you are Lebanese, that in Australia you believe in the workers—'

Without thinking, Helda and I chanted, 'Workers of the world unite, one struggle one fight.'

Mum squeezed my hand tighter and her eyes watered with the effort of containing her mirth.

My father, a member of the Communist Party, presumed Checkpoint Charlie was a place where comrades would eat, drink and recite monologues from Marx or Mao, as they often did when he had his restaurant, Lebanese House. Helda and I knew all the chants – they were a highlight of the May Day marches and of every other protest we were dragged along to on weekends. In Dad's eyes, the revolution was around the corner and we would be the next generation to plot it.

Dad concentrated on lighting his pipe then took a sip of whisky. 'You should begin with: Dear Comrades, every person, everyone here deserves …' He leaned back in his chair. 'No, no, you must begin like this: The bourgeoisie itself, the arch-enemy of the freedom movement …'

That was enough for Mum. She laughed out loud and her shoulders jiggled. She couldn't help it, but she was ruining our chance. If Dad got angry, he could well tear up our voucher. Helda and I stood up at the same time – we had to move quickly.

'So, Dad, we won't be home until one,' Helda said, pulling the voucher out of his grip.

'Wait,' he said.

We froze. Mum was still chuckling in her chair. Dad glared at her before turning to us.

'You must go together. You must stick together.'

Helda let out a theatrical, 'Do I have to?' Then, 'Of course we will, Dad.'

All I was thinking was: one o'clock. We get to come home at one.

'Thanks Dad,' we said calmly and we both leant over and kissed him on the cheek, then we ran down the hallway, our excitement ricocheting off the walls.

We could hear Mum defending herself as she got up to set the table. 'I was laughing at something else. Your daughter told me a joke.' Then I heard her serving our food. She was moving quickly to divert Dad's attention. I could hear him grumbling, but only mildly, so it was likely going to be a peaceful night.

I called Sasha and she was over within ten minutes. The three of us holed up in my sister's room, our hair pulled back off our faces with tight headbands in preparation for our makeover. I sat on the edge of the bed and waited to be painted. Helda stood with a blush brush in hand and looked at my face from different angles, as though it was the first time she had seen me. 'YSL's brought out a new range, golds and orange, I'm going to let you use it. Don't touch, and sit still.' Without looking behind her she added, 'Sasha, stop playing with my lipsticks.'

My eyes watered as I followed instructions: 'Don't blink. Smile. No smile like this. Now turn to the side, close your eyes. Why are your lids fluttering? Close them properly. Pretend you're kissing. Now stretch your lips. Smile. Not like that, smile like this.' Occasionally a wet tissue dabbed in saliva was rubbed against my eyelid or cheekbones, followed by a sigh and 'I'm going to have to start again.'

Then it was Sasha's turn. While I was waiting, I stared at myself in a hand-held mirror with John Travolta's face etched on it. I didn't like what my sister had produced: the pink blush streak across my cheekbones, my eyes red thanks to their multicoloured lids. But if I protested, she would never, ever do my make-up again, for the rest of my life. I told myself to avoid mirrors for the rest of the night. Helda caught me looking at myself and said, 'You look great, you have Mum's high cheekbones, which is good because it helps to balance out your large ears.'

Mum was waiting for us in the kitchen and we knew it would be a waste of time to argue with her. In our big jackets, hiding our outfits, we reluctantly sat and ate the rice, lentils, cucumber and yoghurt. The only one who seemed to be enjoying the food was

Sasha; she loved to eat and Mum loved to feed her. Helda drove and Sasha promised Mum that she would look after us.

When we arrived, Sasha and I threw our warm jackets on the back seat of Helda's car – we didn't want them ruining our look. Freezing in my miniskirt and black sleeveless top, I clung for warmth to Sasha in her vintage silk dress with white, patent-leather, knee-high boots. We stomped our feet to generate some heat, begging Helda to hurry up as she adjusted her large belt, which was wrapped around the white shirt she had borrowed from Dad. She opened the car door and took out her long emerald-green coat. On the lapel was a huge diamond pin studded with plastic stones that glittered.

'Can you see the hole in the shirt now?'

Sasha and I stepped in for a closer look.

'No, it's hidden,' I said. 'Did you just rip Dad's shirt?'

Helda looked striking whenever we went out, but could never maintain the look, not even while we were travelling to our destination. She always somehow developed a rip, hole or stain. Helda grabbed her handbag and took out the voucher, holding onto it tight as she toddled off in her pointy black shoes. 'Come on, hurry up.'

Together we strode towards the club, tugging, yanking and adjusting bits of clothing until the outfits were perfect for our arrival at the door. I realised that for the first time there was silence between us. We must all be nervous, I thought.

There was no crowd to walk past because it was only eight-thirty, way too early for clubbers of Melbourne to be out. Even so, when we got to the door I was still unable to say anything. As we approached the red rope, the doorman raised it for us to walk through and my heart lifted with it. I enjoyed the feeling of being welcomed.

'Thank you,' I said, smiling at the doorman. He didn't smile back.

Once inside, my sister gave me my first nightclub lesson. 'Please don't say thank you to the doorman.'

The three of us stood near the empty dance floor and propped our elbows on a small round table. I looked around at the exposed brick walls and steel spiral staircase leading to a mezzanine area that also looked deserted. Sasha lit up a cigarette and Helda headed towards the bar. There was no point in talking over the music, blasting from every direction and through my entire body. Then, the sound of a trumpet blared, followed by beats that immediately moved me to the middle of the dance floor. I could see the green laser lights even with my eyes closed. When I opened them, Helda and Sasha were there, swishing their arms in the air, and as loudly as I could I sang, *the only way is up*.

MY STORY: THE AFTERMATH OF HAPPENSTANCE

KAYE COOPER

When Mum woke me up to tell me that Dad was dead, my first words to her were 'Are you sure?' I was twelve going on thirteen. My brain, still in that valley between childhood and adolescence, could not grasp the enormity of those words but they were spoken with such anguish I knew it to be true, and so it began.

In the twin bed across from mine, my younger sister slept on. It was pitch black outside, still slick with rain, and two police officers were sitting at our kitchen table. This was the same table that just hours before I had sat at with Dad while he drank instant coffee, before he went out that last time. It was the same table where over the years we had gathered as a family. It was where

Dad told us that there was not enough money that year to pay for rego, and where we heard again and again the stories about the beginnings of us.

Dad was an electrical linesman. He went out into the dark and rain that night to fix a power pole knocked down by a groom, intoxicated after his bucks party. Dad was electrocuted. We were told he screamed. He was only forty. I imagine that cataclysmic moment of death, on that pole, his crucifix, his arms flung wide and his scream splitting the dark. His body too was marked. We could trace the points where the current entered then found its way out to ground. I often think about that bridegroom. I wonder if he went on to get married the next day and if he ever acknowledged the sacrifice of a life for his actions.

Dad's funeral was huge. The Anglican Church at Kingscliff overflowed. Later the funeral procession snaked to the newly created lawn cemetery at Tweed, where Dad's coffin was inched into the ground by an unstoppable mechanical device. It was the new way. It was progress. It was unbearable. After, we feigned alrightness, even with each other. We went on with life, but life was a performance. For a long time after, I searched for Dad in people passing by but he was not to be resurrected.

We lived at Chinderah, before and after. Chinderah, south of Tweed Heads, was a settlement of mostly Aboriginal people and Torres Straight Islanders. My childhood was the colour of sunshine. Even now I can reach in and grasp that ball of warm golden light and feel the rays reflected on my face. We were all just kids together then. It was free and easy days, scrambling over oyster shells to swim in the river, roaming through the bush, climbing trees, and riding bikes we had to stand up to ride because we couldn't reach the pedals. We went to Sunday school and neighbours' parties where, always, someone could play the piano. Fathers worked together to build a hall, mothers catered weddings for the local brides, and together we saw off sons to the Vietnam War.

Chinderah flooded regularly and my sister and I would lie on our bedroom floor and watch the water rise up through the cracks in the floorboards. Dad built our room as a lean-to against the end wall of the original one-bedroom cottage. Dad was denied a bank loan for extensions so had made a few additions himself to the house over the years. When the council building inspector made his rounds one year we held our breath, but he looked at us and said the plan drawings were wrong and promptly pencilled in the extra lines. Inside, our house had curtains for doors and we had an outhouse down the back. We chopped wood and boiled a copper to get hot water for our bath, which we filled with buckets. We had a black and white TV, in front of which I had watched and cried over Kimba the White Lion. In those days we had to pay each year for a TV licence. We paid death duties, and telegrams were feared.

Mum grew up at Chinderah. She was the third of nine children. For most years of her young life she would go to school and when she came home there was another brother or sister to care for. Mum would walk the six kilometres to Cudgen School. Sometimes she would find a horse in a paddock to ride and sometimes she jumped on the rattler that moved cane around the district. On weekends, Mum would walk Wommin Bay Road to Dreamtime Beach and catch worms for the family bait business. She was great at this. She could catch a worm in each hand simultaneously. Mum was smart and wanted to be a nurse, but life took a different turn for her.

Before Dad met Mum, he was a boxer doing the rounds. He must have been good because under the sink in our house, the cupboard was full of trophies.

This pretty much summed up what I knew of my parents' life before us. In an old photo album, stuck in with glue was a black and white photo of a woman sitting at a table with Dad. The woman was beautiful. Mum wouldn't say who the woman was but eventually we figured out it was her, before she was worn down by all of it, back when life still held promise and any number of different paths were open before her.

—

There was no phone in our house and after, when the police left, when we began to work around the edges of our shock and before the tendrils of grief took hold, Mum wanted to tell her friend in Brisbane. We had neighbours that would wake soon, we had relatives to inform, but first Mum needed her friend to know. So I jumped the back fence and used the public phone box. I gave the number for the long-distance call to the operator. Dawn was just starting to colour the sky. The phone rang out. I begged the operator to let me try again but it was only after I choked out the words, 'My dad just died' that I was suddenly connected and I knew this friend would come and help, would comfort Mum and would lift, if just a little, the burden I felt from my shoulders.

There was no WorkCover in those days. Mum got a widow's pension and my sister and I were provided with an Aboriginal allowance for our schooling. I was thankful for the allowance. I was grateful that I wouldn't have to leave school and get a full-time job to help out, because school for me was a sanctuary. Books and learning opened my eyes to the wider world and I wanted to have a place in that world.

This was when I asked again about those stories. My sister was blond and pale and I was red-haired and freckled. My pop, however, who spent his last years in an old caravan in our backyard, was the colour of engine oil, like it had been smeared thinly over his tall, lanky body. My grandfather, who lived next door, in a house on stilts where we slept when our house flooded, was the colour of polished mahogany.

My grandfather's dad had been blackbirded from the South Sea Islands. He was taken by ship to Queensland to cut cane but years later, when policies changed, he was put on another ship to be taken back to the Islands. The terror among the men on board was that they would be dumped at sea, because no-one in authority really knew or cared where they came from, so my grandfather jumped ship, changed his name and became Spanish. It didn't matter that he couldn't speak the language. He had the moustache. He opened a barber shop at Chinderah. I guess he learned to cut hair.

My pop's mum, Rachel, was born in the Ulladulla region. The story goes, a respectable, church-going man came across an Aboriginal girl trying to drown her two 'half-caste piccaninnies' in a river. This white man, secure in his position in life, forded the river at the exact place and time a young Aboriginal girl felt she had no other option but to end the life of her daughters. This chance meeting, this fateful collision of races, caused a meteor of ramifications to hurtle through time, places and futures unknown. This man took the girls home to his wife, who could not have her own children, and they adopted them. One of those girls was Rachel. She married an English free settler and became our great-grandmother, and so the branches of our family were set.

—

In my growing-up time, Aboriginal and Torres Strait Islander people did not have a voice. Indigenous people were still scared and scarred from successive government policies. My mum was always frightened of authority, as she knew what could happen if you didn't follow rules. It was what it was though. At that time, we had no expectations that things would change, that we deserved any better, that anyone owed us anything.

Mum was 'Aunty' to everyone at Chinderah. Over the years, I peeled prawns, picked beans and dug pippies at the beach. Mum and I worked alongside the local women and girls; some we were related to. There was lots of laughter and 'hey cuz' and 'hey sis' call-outs while we worked. I was never 'cuz' or 'sis' though. These were for those who belonged and I was the interloper, the llama amongst the flock. The gossamer threads of my Indigenous heritage were too ethereal to ever grasp. I had no Country. I didn't look or feel Indigenous.

My high school friends were solid, though, and over time secrets were unpacked. One of our friends was gay. The fibre of our society then was built on the wrongness of that but we questioned society, not him. I kept my secret though. These were school friendships separate to my other life. I walked between the two worlds, quietly.

One of the police officers who did the death knock that night kept an eye out for me. Tweed Heads was a small town in those days. If he saw me waiting for a bus to go home after my Saturday job, he would ask how things were going. I think he was concerned I would go off the rails, like many teenagers after a tragedy. He couldn't have been more wrong though. I had my eyes set on a different horizon. When I finished university, I was the local girl who made good and I left it all behind.

My Indigenous heritage, an immovable fact around which I had tried to sidestep for so long, revealed itself when I had my children. They were a beautiful mix of all that had come before. So, I told them the stories my parents had told me. The ripple effects of my forebears' stolen roots can never be reversed. My pursuit for understanding is ongoing. It is an indistinct, long, winding pathway to get back to the beginning, but I acknowledge the custodians of all who have come and gone, those living now and those yet to come whose connection with this land has, is and will always be the core of their being.

In this, my story, are some warp and weft threads of the time of then, of searching for belonging, of life upheavals, choice and tragedy, but also of the acceptance and compassion of strangers, and the richness of life despite poverty.

For my dad.

OUR LULLABY

ESMÉ JAMES

I know when I see the call.

I feel an absence and I know.

No phones in the rehearsal room.

I mutter an apology. Something cold takes possession of me. I leave the room without looking up.

An ethereal song softens behind me. I breathe in what is left of it, warming myself on its words. It talks about happiness, promises of safety. It cools and melts on my lips.

I feel the vibrations. This time I must answer. My voice is a song, warning away a time already passed.

It's your brother.

I hear it and I know.

The church doors crumble as I throw them open. The celestial music flees from the room. Eleven silent faces look on in confusion.

Es, what is it?

I can't answer – shards of ice pierce my lungs, frost is creeping up my throat. *Es?*

Alanah's voice floats somewhere behind me, in another world. She follows me across the room, out into the church carpark. *Talk to me …*

I want to speak but she is in another world. It is winter here and all sound is frozen.

I open the car, fumble the keys into the ignition and reach for the handle. I hesitate. Words find me.

It's Ewan.

The door closes. Alanah knows.

I am disappearing. I am driving. I am looking at the road without seeing. The frost is creeping, devouring the window – my breath fending it away with what warmth remains.

It's going to be okay. He's going to be okay.

The engine is humming. It falls silent.

The door of my house is wide open; I enter, and it is not my house. Something else has taken possession, has drained it. It is not my house.

Before you go in—

I don't listen, I push past Colin, heading for the nucleus of this nothingness. I am coming to find you.

Esmé, he won't wake up. Esmé, he won't wake up.

A mantra – Mum at your bedside, singing. But her words are stifled, suffocated by the room's staleness. Only their ghosts form on her lips. The insipid snowflakes drift across the room, escaping through the open window. They can't survive here.

Mum has faded into washed-out pigments. Only her gaze remains – it's a plea, a call for something. I can't return it, I am unseeing. I only see you. The lifeless body pretending to be you, curled up to one side. You could have been in a peaceful slumber. You could have been dreaming with your eyes wide open – but I can feel the absence and it is suffocating.

I am coming to find you. Sitting by your body, I stroke you, talk to you, pretending I can feel you there. It comforts Mum – she knew I would find you, I always do. At stations, at playgrounds – every time you run away and get lost – down train tracks in the middle of the night I have found you, drenched in the rain. You were standing there, waiting. You weren't scared, you knew I'd always find you.

I am hugging absence.

Blanketing you in my arms, I sing, coming to find you, protecting you. Paramedics arrive but I keep singing.

A seizure, Colin is saying. *I found him shaking … moaning … went cold … nothing like this before … CPR … just stopped moving.*

Your hand in mine, I keep singing – it is our song. You used to skip when I would sing it; your eyes locked on mine as you giggled, flapping your arms in the air. People would stare but you took no notice – you perfectly understood this world that didn't understand you. You would giggle and I would keep singing, flapping my arms with yours in the air.

You are lying motionless and I am singing. The paramedics tell me it's helping – I know they are lying. They have moved you to a stretcher and place a mask over your mouth.

It is not uncommon … keep going … move back to give us room …

A frozen screen hangs above you; cartoon firefighters mercilessly suspended in their moment of struggle are engulfed in a motionless blaze. Who paused it? You had been watching this episode in the morning and I hadn't let you finish it. You were going to be late for school. You flopped back into bed and hid under your covers. You had been giggling while I had been yelling. That memory creeps around my neck and chokes me.

A hand slips into mine, squeezes it – I think it is you. Jim is at my side, stroking me, telling me to keep singing.

The paramedics move around us, speaking in tongues I don't want to understand.

... breathing slowing ... not responding ...

And then I am torn away from you, held back, watching them changing machines, inserting tubes, flicking switches. They won't let me go to you.

Colin tries to hold Mum but she is fighting, screaming – she needs to find you.

I am held and you are taken. Snowflakes are falling, melting in the empty room; nothing survives here.

Jim is holding me, humming in my ear.

... It's okay ... He's going to be okay ...

—

A sterile maze – the smell of disinfectant stifling but unable to mask the rot beneath it. A dull humming fills the air, a nurse starts laughing. The sound is discordant, striking a strained chord with a cry nearby. An elderly lady holds her husband's hand as he stares back, blankly.

I slide down the hospital hallway, sneaking behind curtains, stumbling into moments that were not mine to share. Will they see me in their memories – painted into the corner, a girl who stood there, staring at them blankly?

Sneaking behind curtains, I finally find you, plugged into a machine that is breathing for you. Your pyjamas lie in pieces on the floor – they were red, your favourite. I think that I will sew them back together; I know they will be trashed and burnt.

Mum is reciting the words she has spoken a thousand times.

... autism ... can't speak ... needs help ... all basic needs ... epilepsy ... not like this ... absences ... never shaking ... Will you wake him?

Is this his sister?

Mum looks at me, painted into the corner of the moment.

Yes, his older sister. He loves her more than anything.

I want to feel that everything is okay. We stand frozen, sharing a smile. Something is exchanged, something is invited.

We are with you, hoping – the machine is breathing for you.

There are voices far behind the curtains, approaching, growing louder. My grandparents blunder into our little curtained room.

Nan heads straight over and hugs me. *There, there. Come on, now. No need to think silly thoughts yet.*

Pulling away, she smiles. Her eyes red from crying.

Grandad embraces me and starts laughing. *Do you think he's just trying to get out of school tomorrow?*

That sounds about right. I am laughing. *Did you hear that, Ewan?*

A moment later, Colin and Jim have found us.

A moment after that, my dad.

A voice tells us in the distance, *only one family member in emergency.*

But we cannot hear them, we are laughing. Warm light pools around you.

We make a home in this hospital room.

—

A call wakes me – I think it's my alarm. We have slept and I'm coming to find you. They said they would wake you.

Reaching out, I answer. *Es …*

They are just calling to wake us.

It's your brother … Everything is still okay. *Es …*

I am still sleeping; half asleep, not hearing clearly.

… get here as soon as you can …

I will wake up. I will wake up and we will try again.

They've said we need to say goodbye.

I sit up.

I am awake.

I put the phone down beside me. There is silence.

It is deafening.

I scream.

Not now. Jim lulls me.

He holds me but I am not there, part of me is missing – all of me is missing. I am screaming and you are not there.

Not now. Jim lulls me but I am not there. *Get dressed, get in the car.*

He hands me clothes, he can't find my jacket.

We leave it, it clothes no-one.

Jim is driving and calling my nan; she picks up straightaway.

What is happening? I am pleading.

Nan is silent when she has always been powerful.

I'm sorry, darling.

No-one is laughing.

Drive as safely as you can.

Silence.

A red light, a green light; fading, dying away. The phone rings – Alanah's voice sounds from another world.

Any update? How is he doing?

They said I need to say goodbye.

Silence.

I'm sorry.

At the hospital, I am unseeing – a machine, I am breathing, following signs, running, finding ICU. I am no-one.

My brother. I beg to a nurse. *I need to find my brother.*

She takes me to you.

A knife is sliced through reality – I see through worlds – it is done with words; it has pulverised them, torn the poetry from their meaning. Nothing lives here.

Mum is looking at me, looking up from your body to me. I can see it. Something has been written and I can't change it, I can't make a home in this unreality. We live here now – in a space in between – and we will keep living and you will be absent.

She can't hold me, she isn't there.

A washed-out hand. A mechanical beeping. A window – looking through it, I see my dad. He is running, weeping, holding the falling parts of himself together. He is running across parkland, running through that void, coming to find you.

I clutch at absence.

He is in the room, he is weeping. *My boy, my boy.*

He collapses; his arms try to find you. *My boy, my boy.*

He is melting, cries lacerating the silence. *My boy.*

I pick up his body and try to contain it – it slips through my fingers and pools on the hospital floor.

I can't find you.

Crawling onto the bed, I lie beside emptiness; singing through absence, trying to find you.

—

We are moved, avoided – they don't need us here.

They are talking. When will they kill you? They are checking, consulting. I am singing.

They place a cap over your head – you look like a swimmer. You loved to swim. You would dive right to the bottom and let your body float to the top. You wouldn't lift your head, you'd lie on the surface looking under the water – looking like a body, drowning.

After a while, I would panic, thinking that this time it wasn't a game. And I'd swim towards you, but before I could reach you, your body would flop over and spit water from your mouth, laughing. And I would be laughing, wondering about that strange peace you found there, in the somewhere in between.

They place a cap over your head and no-one is laughing. I am singing, trying to find peace here in absence. Dad is a pool around you. Mum is not there.

They are checking, consulting; they are multiplying, speaking in tongues. I am singing. They are telling me that it's helping – I think they are lying.

I am singing but I've lost sight of the words – I have

forgotten. There is no poetry here.

A sound.

There is something – discordant – and it pierces through this in-between. Mum is singing, catching my words before they slip away. She looks at me and I can feel them. We are singing through absence, coming to find you.

Keep singing. A nurse calls to us, summoning a sea of blue bodies around us. *He can hear you!*

The nurses laughing. The activity in your brain is multiplying. You are responding. You can hear us. You can sense the concert around you.

He's still there!

We are singing, coming to find you.

They tell us to keep singing. So we clutch at notes through laughter. We assemble words and give them meaning; we drift on melodies, flooding the room, drowning in tones and duration. We are finding you. You are here with us. We sing through hours of poetry and meaning, forgetting time and staying beside you. A new day has broken. We can just feel you, the tip of your finger touching me, reaching through this in-between.

There you are.

They will try to pull you over. They are staying, they are deliberating. We must stand back and keep singing. They will pull the tube from you; we will see if you are just machine. You must breathe and keep breathing – we have one chance to pull you from the in-between.

The cord is ripped from you.

There is a silence; we are suspended, drifting somewhere

that time cannot hurt us, swimming through a moment that has no surface. We are emptiness, we are laughter. I hear music.

I hear your laughter.

With a sharp inhale, you rise to the surface. Your eyes flash open, flutter, fade. They are closing. My heart is frozen.

And then, you are smiling. They place oxygen over your mouth. You breathe it. The mask condensates from your warm laughter. Your eyes are blinking, you are searching. They catch mine and there is no fear in your gaze – you were never scared. You knew you would always find me. You hold me there, we are grounded.

The world begins to re-form around us, piecing us back together, making us whole. The doctors are moving around us – they are hugging, cheering. A nurse is crying. You are surrounded and there is music. It is your laughter, singing through spaces, building a bridge through that in-between. I join in your song, laughing. Reaching out, I find you; my hand around yours, soothing you, singing our song of happiness, of promises of safety. Softly, you squeeze back. You are there, I feel you beside me. You are music and you have made it home.

Crawling onto the bed, I hold you in my arms, your body nestling against me. I feel your gentle breathing – you could have been sleeping – your body is flooded by warmth and colour. It spills from you, spreading around our hospital room.

Doctors are parting, performing final checks and procedures. They are speaking to my parents of the future, of possible causes, of preventions. But, for now, I do not hear them. I close my eyes and lie there beside you. I have found you.

And there is a beautiful silence. And it is our song.

BREAKING BREAD

NAEUN KIM

'They're having one of their parties again,' said Mum. 'I'm surprised they can fit all of Lebanon back there,' she grumbled, with a piercing side-eye look only an Asian mother can give.

I squinted through the splintered slits of the wooden fence, to a vista that was a wonderland for an only child – kids running rampant with a soccer ball, vibrant dishes jostling for a spot on the crowded counter, and adults huddled around a barbecue with a heavenly concoction of fat, garlic and spices emanating from the glowing centrepiece.

Mum caught the whiff of my curiosity. 'You know they don't eat pork.' She glanced at my rotund figure. She finished packing my bento box of egg rolls, dried fish, but no garlic.

I resumed my viewing. The children didn't seem to mind missing the final week of term to celebrate whatever they were celebrating, and neither did their parents.

My slog to school would be punctuated by the reassuring clank of our creaky gate and the little corner shop coated in Marjorelle blue. Grey-haired, pot-bellied men puffed and sipped and argued on the makeshift seating outside. Their blaring commentary had become a constant companion to the morning procession – the yelling a precursor to the chaos about to unfold across the street in the school grounds. The men nodded politely at me but it was the table of glistening pockets between them that caught my eye, inside each the fleshy tiers of freshly baked Lebanese bread that seemingly let out a sultry sigh of steam for each passer-by. The school bell rudely interrupted my fantasy and I dragged my feet across the road.

At lunchtime, we would dash to the handball courts to commence our daily debate on which recreational activity would be undertaken. Hide-and-seek won overwhelmingly, cops and robbers a bashful second. This meant we had no time to sit down and eat lunch properly and I was secretly grateful for that.

'Yalla habibi.' Joey beckoned me to the bushes behind the demountables. We called this place, which was dark and dingy, the Forbidden Forest because of its proximity to the boundaries of the street (Healthy Harold made sure we were well versed in stranger danger).

I knew we could get in trouble, but when you're six you tend to follow your heart rather than your head. We spent thirty glorious minutes talking about Miss Russell's haircut and what we were going to bring to show-and-tell tomorrow.

We resumed the conversation on the walk home. Joey lived nine houses down from me on Dudley Street so I would sometimes stay back for some extracurricular eating. Today, the Lebanese bread had been deep-fried in rustic triangular pieces and had a dollop of garlic sauce.

'Salemat yadakhi,' I said, making sure the 'k' sounded like I was clearing my throat.

Mrs Tannous winked at me and I knew I had impressed my future mother-in-law.

I skipped home, full, giddy and armed with a plan: dinner would be ready by the time I bathed, I would then braid some bracelets for show-and-tell and, after Mum had fallen asleep, I'd sneak out of the room to watch *Sex and the City*. It would have to be on mute though, because God forbid Mum should find out I was watching a show with 'sex' in its title.

Mrs Tannous had packed some leftovers and I predicted the garlic dip would work well with our kimchi fried rice. But Mum wasn't in the kitchen. She was pacing around the living room in front of our bulky Panasonic TV that a family friend had been planning to throw out.

'Yalla habibi,' I giggled.

'What does that mean? Where did you learn that from?'

'It's "come here darling" in Arabic,' I gloated, finally knowing something Mum didn't.

On the TV screen was one of the streets Joey and I sometimes meandered through to stretch out the walk home. Some old man in an ill-fitting tweed suit holding a microphone spoke with a contagious concern on his face. That's when I noticed the weatherboard houses and jacaranda trees that usually lined the street had been eclipsed by a flurry of flashing red and blue lights.

'Don't look, just go to your room,' Mum ordered.

I pressed my ear against the door and started writing what I heard in my Winnie-the-Pooh diary. The pages were usually reserved for my parents' arguments, but tonight I wrote about the deadly stabbing of fourteen-year-old Edward Lee on Telopea Street.

I slept with a knot in my stomach that swelled by the hour. In the morning Mum dragged me like an anchor to school, holding her composure as she held my hand. As we turned the corner, I pretended not to notice the three bearded men nodding gently at me. Mum's grip tightened.

'Your dad is going to pick you up today,' she instructed. 'He'll be here by three-thirty. Stay until he comes.'

As I plodded to class I plotted excuses for Dad to drop me off at Joey's after school. Mrs Tannous had promised me pork shish kabobs after I expressed my genuine, yet ill-informed, concern about Joey's porkless diet.

My heart sank when Miss Russell called my name. I could see my half-finished bracelets next to my diary on the desk at home. I pretended not to hear her as I scanned the classroom like a lighthouse. All I could see of mine was my bag with my blue art smock lying languorously on top like one of Picasso's women. It even looked at me with the same nonsensical and chaotic expression, pleading not to be involved in my downfall. I shuffled towards it and promised God I would never watch *Sex and the City* again.

Twelve sets of eyes watched as I unlocked the clasps of my titanium bento box, using each click to buy some time. I pulled the lid off and a blast of sour-chilli-rotten fumes burst out. My face seared red. Reluctantly, I revealed the tackily coiled rubbery egg rolls, morsels of barbie-pink meat, and a glaringly red clump of kimchi. I was always the last to take out my meal at lunch, to save myself from a peppering of questions. The spectators began to holler before I could even think of an Anglo-friendly translation.

'What's that smell?'

'How do you fit so much food in there?'

'Can I try some?'

I looked over at Miss Russell, cross-legged next to Joey at the back, who answered my panicked look with a smile as wide as the Harbour Bridge.

My bento box was handed around with the same buzz and care one exercises in a game of pass the parcel. It was a stunning spectacle – twelve brown-haired, hook-nosed kids marvelling at what they saw: neatly folded egg rolls, bite-size Spam pieces caressed by a frying pan, and the homely handful of spicy, fermented cabbage that brought the meal's denouement to a perfect harmony. All my protesting each morning suddenly seemed puerile and I couldn't wait to go home to tell Mum.

At home time I positioned myself under the towering school sign so even the drunkest of dads would see me. Car by car, I waved goodbye to my friends whose parents lined the gate each afternoon with the same comforting predictability of a taxi rank. Shadows began to lengthen and streetlights flickered on. It was only when the door of Al Houda's mixed business rumbled shut that I began to worry. Its bright blue vigour from the morning had vanished; it avoided my gaze like a student taking cover from a teacher's question. Even its unofficial residents had called it a day, leaving their ornate coffee-stained cups outside to rest until yet another day of storytelling and people-watching. A warm sensation started to fill my pants.

The sprint home was hell. It was like a game of pass the balloon, except the balloon had already popped and there was no-one waiting for me at the other end. The creaky gate was open, so he must still be out drinking. Dad never left the gate closed because he believed in efficiency (or maybe those extra five seconds were better spent at the pub).

When you defy your mother's orders, there comes a moment you realise you should have listened to her. No keys, no phone and by this stage, no common sense. Like a mirage, a grey set of buttons with digits materialised by the door. I had seen it swing open before from Mum pressing it to the tune of 'Mary Had a Little Lamb'. Surely my weekly piano lessons were not just for keeping up with the Kims.

Bad move.

The house started wailing. My cheeks were as wet as my pants. House by house, lights turned on and nosiness, not concern, forced people off their couches. They stood, some with knives tucked behind them, from a distance that allowed for gawking and a chance to run back inside if needed. A flashing blue light blinded the street and the same cars I had seen on Edward Lee's street were now swarmed around mine.

A lady suddenly appeared beside me. Cocooned in a well-worn dressing gown and hair wrapped snug in a damp towel, she had the kind of face that reeked of hardship – wide, unblinking eyes sheltered by two bushy cambers of eyebrows and a solid jawline that looked to have taken a whack from Tom and Jerry's hammer. It was the same brown gown I had glimpsed through the gaps of our fence.

On a night when hands begrudgingly left pockets and steam accompanied the faintest of conversations, she was a welcoming presence. Her coarse hand encased mine as I buried my face in her garlic-scented robe.

Her deep voice sent a gentle rumbling through my body as I nestled my head on her pillowy bosom. The only words I could recognise from the adult conversation were 'alarm', 'mistake' and 'sorry', said at least four times before my eyes fluttered shut.

Muffled voices woke me from my daze. The flashing lights had gone but my neighbour had stayed. My pants were now dry, as were the crusty tears on my cheeks.

'She must be frightened, the poor thing.'

'Yes, the one time I ask her dad to pick her up and this happens. Thank you so much again and sorry for any trouble.'

I pretended to be asleep as Mum picked me up in one arm, her work- and lunch-bags in the other. A car was lurking nearby. It wasn't until we reached the door that a blinding light switched on. Mum had only ever used a taxi once before and my guilt grew as she washed me and tucked me into bed.

—

I woke to a medley of giggles and chortles and bolted out to see who was over, but it was just Mum watering the garden. A steady stream of smoke drifted into our backyard, and by now I had learned that where there's smoke, there's fun. Hose in hand, I replaced my Saturday-morning cartoons with live entertainment, aired through the slits of our wonky fence. White plastic chairs seated the young and old, some with kids on their laps, others with plates spilling over with food. Three boys who looked around my age clung to the Hills hoist as the lady from last night spun them around.

I continued watering. Sometimes, when Mum wasn't looking, I liked to make patterns on the fence. I was mid-swirl when a gentle knock came from the other side. Maybe the fence was doubling as their goalpost today.

'I told you you're wasting water when you do that. And look, now the neighbours are complaining,' Mum snarled.

She snatched the hose from me and went to turn the tap off. Another knock. I looked up and a craggy hand had appeared. The fraying sleeves of a dressing gown followed.

Twinkling in the sunlight, a glossy packet of delicately toasted Lebanese bread dangled above.

FROM LOGANLEA TO LOURDES: A PILGRIMAGE

JACKIE BAILEY

I get the idea at my sister's Confirmation mass. It hits me like a ray of Queensland sunlight, like a semitrailer on the Hume Highway, like the voice of God speaking directly to me.

My sister Allison limps up the aisle and bows her head for the bishop's blessing. She is taking Saint Bernadette as her Confirmation name: the martyr of Lourdes, France, who died of consumption when she was nineteen, but not before she had shaken Christendom to its core with her claims of seeing Our Lady; not before she had been tortured and refused to recant; not before miracles began to occur at the grotto where Our Lady first appeared to her. I shiver in my pew. Just the word 'grotto' sounds like miracles could happen.

After the ceremony we head back home. My sister and I share a double bed, so I wait until she is asleep before I sneak to the toilet. I lean a school exercise book on my knees and write in my best handwriting, Dear Make-A-Wish Foundation, my sister has a malignant brain tumour called an astrocytoma. I am pretty sure of the spelling; I saw it on one of the doctor's letters that Dad keeps in the bill drawer. Her wish is to pray for world peace at the grotto of Our Lady in Lourdes. I tiptoe into the living room and steal a stamp from Mum's purse.

A month passes. It's getting hot enough to run under the sprinkler, giggling and wincing from the bindies. But I don't even suggest it, knowing Allison's leg couldn't stand the effort and I couldn't stand Allison's attempts to keep her tears secret from me. Another month passes; in between his three jobs Dad starts preparing for summer like a man getting ready for a siege, clearing the gutters, burning the leaves in the incinerator in the backyard, checking the garden hose for kinks and leaks. All the Loganlea men are doing the same: summer in the suburbs on the floodplains of the Logan River means bushfires in December, followed by floods in January. Last summer a tree went up in flames across the road from our house at the same time as the creek broke its banks, gushing muddy water down our street.

I am preparing for a different battle. Allison and I used to kneel to say our nightly prayers, but since she got sick we have recited them lying down. Now I return to my knees, folding my hands and keeping my back straight, not leaning on the bed. I won't have this fail because I didn't follow procedure.

My strategy pays off. It's November, three months since

I posted my letter, when Mum answers the phone. 'Oh, wait, I get my daughter,' she says and hands the phone to me; although she is happy to yell at the top of her lungs at her family, Mum doesn't like to talk to strangers on the phone, afraid they won't understand her Singaporean accent.

It's a woman from the Make-A-Wish Foundation, telling me that my prayers have been answered. Millions of Catholics travel to Lourdes each year to drink from and bathe in the miraculous waters. Thanks to Make-A-Wish, the Baileys are going to join them.

We travel for thirty-six hours nonstop to get from Loganlea, Australia to Lourdes, France. We collapse into the beds of our hotel room and the next day Allison, who has been in good spirits for the whole trip, laughs and tells me, 'You sleepwalked last night!'

'Did not!'

'You did! She did, didn't she Dad?'

Dad confirms it; apparently I got up and scrabbled at the door, trying to get out. Before I can protest further, Mum returns. She has ventured into the outside world and come back with rock-hard bread rolls, which is apparently what they eat here in France. I gnaw at mine, imagining a race of people with teeth as sharp as dinosaur incisors, baring them at foreigners with ulterior motives.

After 'breakfast' we leave the hotel and, unsure which direction to go, follow the small groups of people who appear to know the way. No-one looks at us: the white dad, the Asian mum, the cancer girl and the sleepwalker. In this land of pilgrims, we fit right in.

I have to force myself to walk as slowly as the rest of the growing crowd. My mind is an abacus, and I count off the reasons why my sister should be first in line for a miracle. Based on my reading of the lives of saints, I have deduced that answered prayers are about being the right person at the right place at the right time.

Right place: that's easy. Here we are at Lourdes, where Our Lady turned ordinary water into a balm of healing for thousands of believers.

Right person: unfortunately we only have me, and I am pretty far from being the right person for the job. The history of the saints suggests that skinny sick children are at the top of the pyramid, closest to God; then skinny sick grown-ups; then fat sick children; then fat sick grown-ups; and then the rest of us. I can't tell you why skinny and fat matters, but if you read the stories of the saints, which I have done, assiduously making notes, it is obvious that it does. Bernadette: skinny child; Jacinta and Francisco of Fátima: skinny children; Thérèse 'The Little Flower', and Teresa of Ávila: skinny girls; Catholic priest Maximilian Kolbe (by the time he died in Auschwitz): skinny adult.

Anyway, despite being fat from the steroid treatments, Allison is much closer to the top of the pyramid than me. Which makes the fact that she won't pray for herself infuriating. I am hoping that being in the right place will give my prayers the boost that they need to be heard. I am also hoping that God will ignore my recent dabbling with the idea that He might not actually exist. I don't want Him to think I am asking for this miracle as proof. That always backfires.

Right time: this is the hardest part because I cannot know when the 'right' time is. Jesus said that he will come like a thief in the night, so all I can do is be ready. After the sleepwalking debacle, I decide to set my alarm to wake every hour throughout the hours of slumber and say a prayer for Allison so He won't catch me unprepared. During the day I have a prayer for her on repeat in the back of my mind. Please God, may Your will be done. It's important to put it in the hands of God. See, for example, Teresa of Ávila. Occasionally I add a little hint: Please God, may Your will be to heal my sister now.

There are thousands of people in the cathedral and piazza, but the grotto itself is far less busy than I thought it would be. After a wait of only ten minutes, we proceed through a cave that is big enough for an altar, some flowers and about five people at a time. In one nook there is a statue of the Virgin, and a trickle of water cascades from a crevice in the dark rock, which is slick with moisture.

Mum takes some photos of us in the grotto. Afterwards, Allison rests in her hired wheelchair, but I can't sit down anywhere – too young, too healthy – so I shift my weight from left to right, easing one sore footpad and then the other. Mum normally hates seeing Allison in a wheelchair, but in Lourdes she quickly recognises its utility: in this place, if a person isn't in a wheelchair – or better still, a hospital bed – she goes to the back of the queue.

The days pass. We meander at the pace of pilgrims, resting in the shade of trees, going to mass, watching for the coming of Christ and praying. Mum buys dozens of plastic bottles with an image of the Virgin printed on the side and gets me to queue at the wall of taps where people can fill them up with holy water. The lines are dense and people shove and heave their way forwards. I want to yell, You're all supposed to be holy! but I am too terrified to open my mouth. At one point the mob lifts me off my feet and I stumble, grasping for a handhold because I know with dreadful certainty that if I fall, I will die. The woman next to me is old and squat, her hair short and dyed a watery red, and she does not look at me as I pull myself up by her black skirts.

Then it is our last day, the day that we are scheduled to bathe in the water. The day I have been waiting for.

We head to the women's rooms, which are housed in cold grey concrete bunkers. Allison and Mum are directed to the section reserved for the sick and dying. I had not expected to go in alone and I want to run after them, but a small nun in a grey veil holds my elbow and gestures for me to follow her. Inside the bunker stands a row of large, grey concrete baths filled with holy water pumped direct from the source.

The nun doesn't speak English but it is clear what she wants me to do as she points to my dress and then makes a sweeping motion with both her hands. I strip off and shiver, trying to cover my breasts and small bush of pubes, but the nun is completely indifferent, intent only on grasping my arm and leading me to the tub. This is an industrial-scale operation, shuttling thousands of pilgrims through the icy water every day. I had imagined lying back, letting the water cleanse me. Instead I wade through it as fast as I can, the water so cold that it knocks the breath out of me, and I cannot for love, money or even my sister actually submerge my body in it. The nun titters, but not unkindly.

I meet Allison and Mum outside. Allison is still limping. I try to believe that miracles are not always instantaneous but in that moment I feel my faith crumble into motes of dust, because God should be capable of magic in the service of reason.

As I look back now on our family's unsuccessful trip in search of a miracle, I wonder if perhaps Allison really was closer to the top of the pyramid: perhaps it was her prayers, and not mine, which were fleetingly answered.

After she, Mum and I had bathed in the holy waters, Dad emerged from the men's bathing rooms and met us at a bench by the banks of the river. The church bells tolled, and a choir singing 'Ave Maria' dispersed the clouds above our heads, blowing our petty selves away like so much unnecessary debris.

'This is my favourite hymn,' Dad said.

We all listened, even Mum, who was not a baptised Catholic, who was typically incapable of sitting still without a pen and a racing guide in her hands. The music washed all the fears and dislikes out of me. Mum doled out pieces of ham and baguette for lunch. Dad stood before us, looking somehow taller and lighter than normal. Allison sat in her rented wheelchair, accepted the proffered sandwich with her good hand, and ate. Maybe this was all she had ever really wanted: not a trip to Lourdes, or even a cure for cancer, but a moment of peace with her family.

JUST DANCE

MICHAEL SUN

The year was 2008, and I was going to a Catholic primary school called St Patrick's. It was a tiny school, with three flat brick buildings, one class per grade, and an outstanding number of students who later turned out to be gay. I don't think my parents would have sent me to St Patrick's if they'd had access to a crystal ball whose only function was to determine the future likelihood of any given person's queerness but, then again, I don't quite know why my parents sent me there at all.

Apparently, they had decided early on in my life that I was to go to a Catholic school even though they were first-generation Chinese migrants who were not Catholic, had never been Catholic and didn't know anyone who was Catholic. They didn't go to church, and didn't even want me to go to church. Once, when I was desperate to fit in, I begged my parents to take me to mass after Sunday cartoons and my dad reluctantly obliged. We went, and we sat in the chairs, and then we left, and my dad asked me if I wanted to come back to church again or whether I wanted to keep watching cartoons next time, and I said cartoons and that was the end of it. It turned out the only thing I wanted more than fitting in was to watch *The Fairly Odd Parents* at ten-thirty am on Sundays.

I think my parents sent me to Catholic school to get 'discipline', and they eventually took me out of the school because as an eleven-year-old I was getting too disciplined in matters of faith and not enough in matters of academia. What could I say? I loved Jesus or, more accurately, Jesus' body, by which I mean the Eucharist and not his actual body; okay, maybe some depictions of his body, where you can practically see his abs rippling across his torso, but definitely not the one hanging above the altar of St Patrick's Catholic Primary School church in 2008, where his abs were, granted, rippling but also obscured by red paint (aka blood), to the extent that they were no longer visible except in the semi-hidden, teasingly coy way of someone who answers the door in a bathrobe.

I was not attracted to Jesus, but one person I was attracted to, or attracted to in the pre-puberty sense of wistfully staring at someone and willing them to spend all their time with you – which I guess is exactly the same way I am still attracted to people – was M, a boy one year older than me who had the same first initial as me, which I always wanted to point out and turn into an inside joke but never could, because someone sharing their first initial with you is neither rare nor romantic.

I met M at after-school care, which took place in a large hall at a public school about ten minutes' bus ride from St Patrick's. M actually went to St Patrick's too, but we never saw each other during school hours, only afterwards in this very large and very fluorescently lit hall. Sometimes it felt like we were co-workers having a clandestine affair, except we were an eleven- and a twelve-year-old who were not having any sort of affair, let alone a clandestine one – only, if I was lucky, a shared bus seat on the ten-minute ride to after school-care, during which we would not talk to each other at all.

I always associate different crushes of my life with the songs that came out while I was head over heels, and for M, it's 'Just Dance' by Lady Gaga, a song about getting *half-psychotic sick hypnotic*. I don't think a single thing happened in 2008 that isn't now soundtracked by 'Just Dance' in my memory, like staring at the Jesus above the altar of the St Patrick's Catholic Primary School church with 'Just Dance' playing in the background, or being punched in the stomach by Cassandra Bonfa with 'Just Dance' playing in the background, or being forced to join M's cult with 'Just Dance' playing in the background.

When I say forced, it was more like my own pre-pubescent crush forcing me to join M's cult, so what I really mean is I joined M's cult for love. When I say cult, though, what I really mean is cult.

M had the kind of charismatic personality that only a queer person could have, as in he was loud and attention-seeking at a time when I was also loud and attention-seeking but didn't really know how to make people believe that being loud and attention-seeking could be charismatic rather than deeply annoying. Sometimes when I think about M, I think I might be getting the story wrong, and that everyone maybe did think he was deeply annoying, but then I remember that he convinced ten people to join a cult, and if that isn't charismatic I don't know what is.

This cult was centred entirely around a rejection of technology, making M the youngest boomer ever, or potentially the real identity of Banksy. I have no idea how the cult started, just that I was enticed into it as part of M's master plan to form a critical mass – his logic was that once a certain number of people had joined the cult, the other students at after-school care would have no choice but to join the cult, unless they wanted to be part of a minority, which no-one wanted. (Actually, I was already a minority, since I was a fervent Little Monster – which is what every Lady Gaga stan in 2008 called themselves and still calls themselves – so M and I both knew the unspoken reason I was joining was because I was in love.)

Obviously, I didn't need much convincing to join the cult. All it took was one tap on the shoulder from M and I was in, I was in deep. I would gladly have betrayed anyone I knew if it made M happy or even satisfied. M was my king in the medieval sense, where I would have gladly been his court jester, which is really just a roundabout way of saying I was a clown.

Every afternoon at after-school care M would come around and check on us, to make sure we were not using any form of technology at all, that we were not playing snake on our Nokia phones, or so much as watching other people play Mario Kart on the Nintendo 64, and definitely not listening to 'Just Dance' on our iPod Nanos. I guess that was the point of the whole shebang – something about unplugging and digital detox and rest and relaxation, although I doubt even M, child prodigy though he was, would've framed it in such alluring buzzwords. We had weekly meetings where we didn't talk about much, or perhaps I was just distracted, because for the entire duration of the meeting I would be wistfully staring at M and willing him to spend all of his time with me.

On sunny days M would have us gather, all ten of us, or maybe it was even more towards the end, up on the grassy knoll above the very big school hall, like Children of the Corn. I am imagining him now in a white robe, but I am certain what he was actually wearing was a grey shirt with a blue and yellow striped tie and grey shorts and knee-high socks, which was also what I was wearing and was the school uniform of St Patrick's Catholic Primary School. On the grassy knoll we would hold hands, free from the shackles of technology – no Nokia phones or Nintendo 64s or iPod Nanos with 'Just Dance' the only song loaded onto them – distracting us from what was in front of our very eyes, which at that moment in time was M in the centre of the circle. Sometimes he would deliver what I would now call a sermon.

There's one line I remember most clearly, because he said it again and again on different days – he said 'technology rots your brains', which was meant to strike fear into our hearts and make us never use technology again, but what he didn't know was that my brain was already rotten and the only thing left in it was the song 'Just Dance' by Lady Gaga.

Sunny days like these were the most cult-ish but also the most blissful, and those days make me understand the addiction of religion in a way that no amount of Catholic teachings ever could. M's charisma – or his loudness and attention-seeking disguised as charisma – was addictive in a way that being with him felt like permanently having ingested half a badly measured edible, like I was galaxy-braining towards him, my king, at the centre of that circle and also every circle. He was addictive in a way that made me forget about 'Just Dance' by Lady Gaga, even if just for a moment.

I think that's why, when I saw him a decade later, five Lady Gaga albums later, I didn't even recognise him. He had become a blur in my memory. In my mind, he was no longer real – just a rush, a peak that I had been coming down from my whole life. I didn't think I would ever see M again, even though deep down I always hoped I would, even after we had both left after-school care, even after we had both moved schools and long since stopped talking to each other.

When I saw M again I was at the university pub and he was in Young Labor, which makes total sense for someone who was loud and attention-seeking and had also started a cult. If early-2010s indie cinema had taught me anything, it was that if you go searching for an old flame all you will find is someone married with kids who has no intention of rekindling their relationship with you, and you will end up sad and alone.

But what I found wasn't someone married with kids – it was someone who was twenty-one and queer, which was somehow … worse. Plus, I was sad and alone anyway.

If M had been married with kids, I would've known that my eleven-year-old fantasy was just that, a fantasy. But what I imagined might have happened between M and me now felt like something more, as if the fact that he'd turned out to be queer meant that more *could* have happened, as if it validated my pre-pubescent crush and those hours of wistfully staring at him, as if his wild anti-technology cult was suddenly the most reasonable, blissful thing in the world again.

I thought all of these things, even though when I saw M again I knew I was no longer attracted to him. He told me he had no memory of the cult, but when we talked I quietly hid my phone under my bag, just in case.

THE DARKNESS

CAITLYN DAVIES-PLUMMER

Maybe the darkness began when I was five years old?

The recess bell rang abruptly and echoed throughout the classrooms across the school. Within minutes the schoolyard resembled that of headless chickens running in every direction. Chasey was a firm favourite at recess, except on this day the kids weren't playing chasey. On this day they were playing 'run away from Caitlyn'.

After what felt like an eternity, they finally stopped. They circled around me like hyenas about to attack their prey. Little Johnny proudly took a big step out of the circle towards me. Johnny was a blue-eyed, blond-haired kid who probably had a touch of ADHD and always sounded like he was yelling. He began shouting and laughing, 'No-one wants to play with you. We all know you're dirty and don't have baths!'

Immediately, a chorus of giggles echoed around me. I looked around at the circle, really confused. My young brain couldn't comprehend why this snotty kid was accusing me of not having baths – my parents made me have a bath every night! After a long pause, I finally worked up the courage to reply. 'I have a bath every day! I'm not dirty!'

Johnny pointed at my arm. 'Look at your skin. It's so brown and dirty. You don't look like any of us.' He then lined his arm up against mine. 'See, you're definitely dirty. It's much darker than mine.'

I immediately turned and ran away, not wanting them to see me cry.

I remember coming home and asking Mum why the other kids thought I was dirty. I wanted to have a bath, to just wash my skin colour away. I needed to scrub until I couldn't scrub anymore, but I couldn't wash my colour away and I evidently couldn't keep the darkness away either. Did the darkness start then?

Depression is a really strange illness. No-one can see it, but it feels like you're slowly drowning on the inside. It's a darkness that envelops you, rendering you unable to ever see light. Unable to ever think things could get better, or that you deserve them getting better. I don't think there is a word for depression in any Aboriginal language. Yet our mob has some of the highest suicide and depression rates in the world. I never understood depression until I lived it. I don't think anyone truly can. But at this point I've had it for so long, it feels like a really mean friend who won't take the hint and leave. I'm fearful for what will happen if it leaves me one day. I don't think I'd know myself without it anymore.

Maybe the darkness began when I was ten years old?

Physical education was never a lesson that I looked forward to. Not being blessed with a high level of coordination, I played goal shooter in netball so I didn't have to run. On this particular day we were learning the art of sprinting.

The hundred-metre sprint was the first race, and as I stood at the starting line I could feel my heart beating through my chest. Every thump was pounding in my ears and I could have sworn everyone else could hear it too. I knew I would come last. I was just hoping that no-one would notice.

The PE teacher strutted around like he was an Olympic coach. He tried to ignite a competitive spirit in kids that were just never going to have it. The man had a starting gun, for goodness sake. We were just a bunch of ten-year-old kids.

Bang! The gun went off to start the race, scaring the shit out of a bunch of girls, and their combined screams were louder than the shot itself. Obviously and not surprisingly, I lost the race. My running style was similar to a baby giraffe taking their first steps in the world. In fact, the baby giraffe would probably be more graceful.

After we had all crossed the finish line, I heard a voice shout out, 'I thought she was Aboriginal, isn't she meant to be fast?' Again, a chorus of laughter immediately followed.

I wanted the earth to swallow me and to become invisible. I had to make a quick decision on what my reaction would be and I chose the only safe option. I decided to laugh along with everyone else, quickly wiping my eye, trying to hide the single tear that was running down my cheek. *Did the darkness start then?*

Depression stays with you wherever you go. It isn't something you can just switch off. It feels like you're carrying a hundred kilos of weight around on your shoulders, without ever being able to put it down. Every face that looks at you is judgemental.

Maybe the darkness started when I was twelve?

Canberra was the family holiday destination that year. As you can imagine, my twelve-year-old self was not overly ecstatic about the idea of a holiday in the nation's capital.

After a few riveting days of city tours and museums, my parents decided to take us to Parliament House. The day was classic Canberra weather: cool, windy and dreary. The clouds covered the sky, with only small hints of sunlight coming through. My sister and I dragged our feet towards the entrance to Parliament House, thinking that with each loud stomp we were making a loud protest about the day's agenda.

At this time, the Aboriginal Tent Embassy was standing loud and proud out the front of Parliament House. There were two women walking in front of us as we approached the entrance. We overheard them discussing their views on Aboriginal people very loudly. 'What a bunch of ungrateful, dirty dole bludgers,' one of them said to the other, pointing at the tents.

The other woman nodded her head in agreement and replied, 'Yeah, what are they complaining about? They get everything handed to them, and then spend it all on alcohol and drugs. How are they allowed to sit there like that? It's so unappealing to all the visitors to Parliament House. They should be arrested.'

We followed them to the lift, standing quietly behind them. The tirade continued for a few more seconds and then one of them caught sight of me, my dad and my sister out of the corner of her eye. Both of the women turned around.

'Oh my god! I am SO sorry. We didn't realise you were behind us,' the first woman gushed, visibly going red and looking decidedly embarrassed.

The second joined in. 'We definitely weren't talking about you. You're the good ones. We just mean the drunks and drug addicts,' she nodded to herself, as if satisfied with her intellect and ability to backtrack.

They both clearly thought they had covered their tracks really well. We all just stood there in shock with awkward, uncomfortable smiles on our faces. What were we supposed to do? Make an even bigger scene? That would only prove their point about trouble-making Aboriginal people. So we did what I've done my whole life – we nodded and forced a laugh out. We sat with our own pain and pushed it to the side to make *them* feel comfortable about the racist words they had said. Did the darkness start then?

I don't have enough words to explain every act of racism I have been subjected to in my life. But through all of that, I was able to coexist within my darkness. We tolerated each other. I knew it was there, but I could still push it to the side and function. Until one day, I just couldn't anymore.

After my son was born, I suffered a traumatic postpartum injury. Those magical first five months of my son's life are a blur. I don't remember him being a newborn. I don't remember cuddling him for hours on the couch. I don't remember his first smile.

All I remember is being in pain.

All I remember is kneeling on all fours next to his bassinet, trying my best to rock it back and forth because I couldn't physically stand up. Trying to stop myself from crying too loudly by placing my hand over my mouth in a failed attempt to muffle the sounds coming out.

I remember having to stop in the middle of a breastfeed to go to the toilet, leaving my newborn baby in his bassinet crying his little lungs out for more milk. I remember sitting on the toilet for thirty minutes in complete agony, while listening to my baby scream for me, feeling completely helpless and screaming myself. I felt like a complete failure as a mother.

During those five months, I was let down by the medical system, the doctors, the surgeons. The people who I trusted to help me did not. The physical pain only came to an end after we drove five hours from Adelaide so I could get the operation I needed done by a surgeon in country Victoria. Within two days of the operation, I could finally sit down. I could go to the toilet with little to no pain. I felt like I could breathe again. The light that I couldn't see for so long was back.

For two months after my surgery I lived my life in bliss. I was so thankful to not be in pain anymore, to be able to look after my child. I was experiencing life within a happy bubble. Everything tasted better, everything smelt better, life was finally full of colour. The bubble was so beautiful, my baby was so beautiful, and I never thought that the bubble would burst. Until one day it hit me. The darkness hit me in a way I'd never been hit before. The bubble burst and the darkness set in.

I pushed through for a few weeks after the darkness returned. But I could only hide it for so long, until one day I couldn't. I was checked into a mental health unit for mothers with babies – somewhere I never imagined myself ending up in. They diagnosed me with PTSD as a result of my postpartum injury. But the health unit was not as scary as it sounds and it's definitely not like in the movies. It felt a little bit like camp but with medication and a lot of therapy. After six weeks of intense therapy for two hours every day and a nurse to look after me 24/7, I was discharged and left to fend for myself. Alone.

I functioned for a few weeks, but a month after my discharge I was ready to kill myself.

I wanted to stop the constant feeling of failure. I wanted my son to have a better mum, my husband to have a better wife, my family to have a better daughter. I didn't want this darkness anymore. As soon as I woke up that day, I knew the darkness had become too heavy to carry. I was tired. I didn't feel like I had anything left in me to give. I couldn't keep fighting. The darkness had won.

My husband took my son for the day and I stayed with my parents. As the day wore on, I slipped further and further into my depression. I made a plan. I devised an escape. Relief immediately washed over me. I packed the car. I didn't even bother putting clothes on but stayed in my pyjamas. I went to walk out the front door and my mother stopped me. Her eyes filled with tears as she grabbed my arm. 'Are you okay to drive?' she asked, terrified of my answer.

In that moment I had a choice. I could have lied. I could have said I was fine and continued on with my plan. But I used the one ounce of energy I had left, dropped to floor and began hysterically sobbing.

The decision I made that day determined the direction the rest of my life would take, including whether it would have any direction at all. The depression and the darkness is still with me. Every day it's a battle I fight. But I know my ancestors are warriors and I believe their strength still lies deep within me.

Maybe I'll never truly know when the darkness started. And maybe that doesn't matter. But I do know the moment I decided to fight back. Letting other people carry the weight allowed it to not feel so heavy. I may be coexisting with depression but I know that, with my family, my mob and my ancestors behind me, I will never allow it to win.

LION LIES

HUGH JORGENSEN

I have started lying on official forms that ask 'are languages other than English spoken in your family home?' This deception began when I learned the 'non-English language' question provides one of the few data sets employers have for measuring the 'non-Anglo' make-up of their workforce. Now, whether it's the census, work forms or dating-app surveys, I deliberately fudge my answer to avoid triggering klaxon alarms wired deep into my subconscious by my Singaporean Chinese mother.

—

'I've booked you as lion dancers for the Singapore Club of Queensland Chinese New Year dinner!' Mum beamed, to me, eleven, and my sister, eight. 'Aunty June from the club is coming over to see you both dance, so make Mum proud.' Evidently Mum had promised June, a Singapore Club powerbroker, that we were not only proficient lion dancers, but were also available for public and private shows. Having done very little in a lion costume beyond tripping over, this was all fairly surprising news. But with Mum just newly elected to the plum position of editor of the Singapore Club newsletter, the family name was in too deep to reverse course.

—

I began lion dancing at age nine, a year before our family moved to Australia. We were then living on the outskirts of a farming town in New Zealand. Specifically, the Waimumu crossroads, population: our family.

The four corners of the crossroads contained an abandoned school, an abandoned town hall, an abandoned Presbyterian church and our house. Interaction with other humans in Waimumu was limited, let alone with anyone else of Asian descent. Starved for contact with melanin-rich folk, Mum would bundle me and my little sister into an old white Honda and slam the accelerator for two hours each way every Saturday in order to get us to lion-dancing classes at the nearest Chinatown, in Dunedin.

Our after-class reward was a few slices of roast pork dripping in Char Siu sauce from the Asian minimart below the dancing school. I didn't need the bribe. As someone of hybrid ethnicity, putting on a lion-dancing costume already afforded a niche kind of freedom.

A full-sized lion costume comprises two main parts: a large, lacquered papier-mâché head that fits over your own, and a tail. Inside the head, the lion pilot has access to two sets of wires: one for waggling the lion's ears; the other for fluttering its eyelids like a flirtatious Looney Tunes character. There is also a hand-operated mouth flap for mock-devouring anything from toddlers' noses to heads of lettuce containing those famous red packets of wealth and good fortune (usually about five dollars or, if you're lucky, a scratchie). Like the rear end of a pantomime horse, the lion tail requires a second performer with an affinity for hunchbacked dancing. The whole thing is covered in technicolour fur, sequins and little jangly sewn-in bells.

Performing inside such an instantly recognisable symbol of Chinese culture, I figured any audience member could only assume I was a 'proper' Chinese kid, rich in the culture of his ancestors like ... Mulan and ... one of those Emperor guys. No observer could know that it was merely me, a biracial mudblood, dumb in Mandarin and more steeped in the lore of R.L. Stine's *Goosebumps* series than in his own mother's heritage.

This isn't a slight on Mum, who was forever devising strategies for us to feel pride in our ethnicity. But for half-Chinese kids in a white-majority country, her struggle was never-ending. I had already learned that the easiest way to outwit kids in the playground who were chanting 'ching chong chinaman' and tugging at their eyelid corners, so as to upset my concentration during a keepsies game of marbles, was to neutralise my 'Asianness' by foregrounding my white heritage. This basically meant boring classmates into submission with stories I thought appealed to whiteness, like how Dad's father was a Gallipoli veteran, and my love for McDonald's thirty-cent ice creams.

—

Aunty June was the sort of woman who only ever sat at right angles. When she arrived on that sweaty Brisbane summer afternoon to appraise our lion-dancing proficiency, she poised herself on the edge of our cracked pleather sofa for fear of being caught reclining and melting into the couch.

'Do you have air-conditioning?' she asked.

'Yes, of course,' said Mum, and, turning to me, 'put it on dear', knowing full well our air-conditioner was broken and the sound of its impotent whimpering fan was at best a placebo.

June, fanning herself with the latest Singapore Club newsletter, interrogated us: 'Where did you learn to lion dance?'

'Dunedin.'

'Where?'

'It's in New Zealand.'

—

Mum had tried to teach us Mandarin, but quickly found it was hard enough keeping her five offspring from sticking forks into live power sockets, or each other, let alone passing on a second language. Plus, we were linguistically lazy, evident in that I only absorbed two words. The first was 'Popo', pronounced a bit like 'paw paw', which is sort of slang for 'mother's mother'. When Mum was feeling flush enough to make a long-distance call back to her mum in Singapore, she would have us line up like motley soldiers in our hand-me-down clothes and shout 'Hello Paw Paw!' down the receiver of a red rotary phone that predated the Cold War.

The only other word connecting me to three thousand years of Chinese linguistic evolution was 'fangpi', Mandarin for 'fart'. Mum forbade 'fart' and only permitted the usage of its supposedly less vulgar translation. Dad manipulated this edict to great comedic effect, and on a gusty day in the lounge would giggle 'Sorry, I fangpi'd!', upon which we would all roll about on the floor hooting 'Fangpi! Fangpi!' as Mum's eyes rolled out of her head and crashed through the floorboards on their way to the other side of the earth.

So for all my childhood, the 'Mandarin for kids' books that Mum bought with her meagre nurse's pay cheque sat forlornly on our bookshelf in their original shrink-wrap, like a flock of albatrosses just dying for a neck to hang off.

Undeterred, Mum was always on the lookout for Chinese cultural events (where we could sometimes rub shoulders with kids who had two Chinese parents), regularly cooked all the Chinese dishes she could remember and, eventually, enrolled us in lion dancing.

Sadly, it didn't take long to find that my sister and I were about as good at lion dancing as most Australian prime ministers are at professional-grade cricket, which is to say our performances were at best hesitant and at worst somehow sort of sad. Highly trained lion-dancing troupes draw heavily upon Kung Fu movements to bring the story of a family of mummy, daddy and baby lions to life, utilising choreography that wouldn't look out of place at Cirque du Soleil. Seeing our collective inability, the instructors instead assigned us the role of baby lions. This meant donning a runty one-person lion suit which exuded big participation-award energy.

—

Sizing us up, Aunty June asked, 'Do you have a routine?'

'Umm, sort of, but we haven't done it in a while.'

Mum shot us a threatening glance.

'But I reckon we can still do it! Although we only ever danced as baby lions, and we don't have our own costumes.'

'You don't have costumes?'

'No but like, we can mime some for you?'

Aunty June hmmmed. She pulled a cassette from her purse with 'lion dance music' scrawled on its cover and handed it to my sister.

'Let's see what you can do.'

——

In mid-1997, a few months into lion-dancing lessons, Mum's years-long inception of Dad to emigrate to Brisbane bore fruit. Mum was elated – it would be warmer there, she assured us, we would no longer be the only Asians in town, and there would be a suburb called Sunnybank where the streets were basically paved with Char Siu pork.

Although registered from birth as a citizen of Australia, I didn't know much about it, and began devouring any information about my new home, including a news report on New Zealand's Channel One about the rise of Pauline Hanson's One Nation Party. Hanson was the first Australian politician I learned about. I recall a distinct tightness deep in my gut about moving to a country where someone so opposed to immigrants who looked like me or Mum could have such rabid support.

That said, being an instinctive battler, Mum was very quick

to prove Pauline's prophecy about local jobs going to Asian (via New Zealand) immigrants true. In a career shift, Mum became a solicitor at a small family law office in Ipswich, the epicentre of Hanson's Oxley electorate.

Being an election year, wandering through Ipswich mall to pick up Mum meant passing corflutes stamped with Hanson's face, buying Chupa Chups from a man behind a glass countertop decorated in One Nation Party bumper stickers, and having Dad slap our arms down if we jeered at anything pro-Pauline: 'Not so loud! We'll get beaten up!'

But even in Queensland in the late nineties, Pauline was already howling into the wind. To me, straight out of the Waimumu crossroads, Queensland didn't just have swamps of Asians, it had whole estuaries, rivers and seas of them. Australian–Asians didn't even seem to band together as 'Asians' by default, but just as breezily defined themselves by particular ethnicities or specific places of origin, rather than the amorphous 'Asia' of 3.5 billion people and some fifty countries. They didn't go to 'Asian' supermarkets, but to Vietnamese grocers, Korean butchers and Indian spice bazaars.

—

My sister put the bootlegged cassette into our stereo and hit play. Like gymnasts bound for the gallows, we assembled at the corner of our lounge's four-by-five-metre patch of brown '70s-hangover carpet and waited for the music to start or, one better, for child-services paratroopers to blast through the ceiling and extract us to freedom. We had considered practicing beforehand but given we didn't know any actual moves to rehearse, agreed we may as well just improvise.

The familiar boom! boom! boom! of the drums blared through the speakers, followed by the arrhythmic crash! crash! crash! of the cymbals.

Lion dancing's weakest element is by far the backing soundtrack, which to my (admittedly untrained) ear sounds a bit like some cymbal- and drum-playing wind-up monkeys have come to life and then developed a tragic addiction to meth. Amid such cacophony, where to even begin?

We had nothing.

June raised an eyebrow at Mum, whose eyes darkened.

But at the second round of BOOMs, realising that our, and more importantly our mother's, Singaporean credentials were on the line, I strode into the carpeted arena. I began high-kicking and punching my hands in the air to each BOOM, mime-jerking my imaginary lion's head up and down. Though my lead was more donkey than lion, my sister bravely set off in tow beneath the war-weary eyes of our grandfather's portrait, inventing her own flailing moves as she advanced upon our living room's second ridge.

BOOM CRASH BOOM.

Too far gone to be encumbered by shame, we started leaping about, hoisting our imaginary lions' heads as high as our pre-adolescent arms could reach.

CRASH BOOM BOOM CRASH.

We began doing barrel rolls. Lions don't do barrel rolls, but absent the restraints of real-world costumes, our mime baby lions were free to push the conceptual limits of the art form.

Mid-roll, I glanced at Mum, expecting to see eyes filled with horror at our desecration of the lion dance.

Instead, I saw a toothy smile.

She was, after all, watching her small kids making fools of themselves for her sake, and to show they were worthy of being mid-dinner entertainment at a gathering of 150 drunken Singaporeans at a cheap Chinese restaurant on the Pacific Motorway.

The weight of those 'Mandarin for kids' books tugging at my neck lifted a little.

The BOOMs were reaching crescendo point. Time for the big finish. For Mum. For our ancestors. To give the mid-finger salute to those schoolyard crumbums who psyched me into losing my most valuable marbles, and a double barrel for Pauline.

Forward roll, side break, pivot, neck roll, mime-lion-head to the ancestral heavens!

Scott and Fran in the '92 *Strictly Ballroom* finale, me and my sister in a South Brisbane living room in the '98 improv-mime-lion-dancing championship. These are the two great Australian dance moments of the '90s.

Aunty June grinned. 'I'll get the club to order two baby lion outfits.'

—

As it happens, I am now taking Mandarin classes for my job, and a few weeks ago I sustained my longest ever conversation in Mandarin with Mum, for a total of forty-five seconds. But even if I never crack a full minute, in answering 'is a non-English language spoken at home?', I intend to continue propagating the falsehood of 'yes'. In my defence, this lie does normally generate a follow-up request to 'select any non-English language(s) spoken at home', which gives me the chance to scroll through a drop-down menu of all known mother tongues until I can click on a kind of approximate truth: 'other'.

OUTSIDERS

DIANNE USSHER

Sydney. Bedlam. Everything I didn't do: buildings, buses, cars and crowds confined within concrete surroundings. I found the address. I lit a cigarette and tracked my eyes over the street, crawling with suits, sandwiches in hand. Different peoples, different cultures. I questioned my place as an Aboriginal here. How many of Australia's diverse cultures acknowledge us as the Traditional Owners?

I grew up unaware of my Aboriginal ancestry and history until my aunty unearthed the truth. Secrets born of fear and shame. I see my mother and grandfather, all my aunties and uncles before me, and wonder how I didn't know. Mum had dark hair, thick, wavy and long. I think that's why Dad called her a black bitch.

I traced my mind through the then and the now. Each year, each cycle, had changed me and readied me. I was here for mediation day. My case was against the organisation I had worked for.

—

I grew up in Lismore in the 1960s. It was a country town that harboured an 'us' and 'them' mentality. I was an 'us' because I belonged to the majority. The black people were the minority, they were the 'them' and 'lazy to boot'. The black people lived on the outskirts. My family moved into a large, high house at the beginning of a street, the roadway into the fringes. I'd watch the black people walk past our house, down the long road empty of other homes, and wonder where they were going. There was nothing beyond my place, so where did they belong? I couldn't recall being told to be afraid, but I was. My ears rang consistently with adult voices, 'You can't trust that black bastard; look at that drunken black bitch walking down the road with her shifty kids, they're filthy mongrels, all of them.' Outsiders. Not welcome here.

—

Peter and Paul, my first boyfriends in kindergarten, danced in my mind's eye while I waited in the Sydney sun. They were small twins with black skin and white parents, their short, thick black fringes falling loosely over foreheads that didn't manage to hide sad brown eyes. My pretty and fun best boyfriends who, with smiling white teeth and speedy legs, would chase me in the playground. Somehow, in my childlike mind, we were the same. They had white parents like me, so I didn't know otherwise.

Hindsight is precious. Were Peter and Paul separated from

their family and culture? I am not able to reflect upon those years without seeing the cycle of Stolen Generations, the present and not just the past. The Traditional Owners of Australia, not welcome. A culturally diverse country intent on crumbling the culture of its owners.

The glass doors opened into a cold concrete void painted beige and grey. My faith and that of my Dharug ancestors guided me through, letter in hand. I was dressed flash. Black, red and gold pinstripe pants, white shirt and yellow sandals. Walking on sunshine, no bastard can beat me.

The thirty-fourth floor was a large chamber with a giant illuminated screen on the wall, characters flashing upon it just like an airport departures board. Instead of countries, times, terminals and gate numbers, it scrolled through names, times and mediation room numbers. Trying to trick me into thinking I was going on a holiday. My name appeared. Dianne Ussher versus the State of New South Wales. Mediation Room 7, twelve pm. The State of New South Wales? No wonder I'm so fucked. How hadn't I connected the organisation with the State? Significant oversight.

The directions to my solicitor were simple. No hush money, creative rights to write and visually tell my story, and my painting – a work painted under duress as a return-to-work plan and currently hanging in their head office – returned to me. I could feel it weep, just as I was. No painting, no deal. Not too much to ask after five years of psychological dissection. One way or another, I'd peel the carpet back and bare all they'd swept there. Bullying, discrimination, and a questionable mandatory report that had resulted in the removal of an eight-month-old Aboriginal baby from his mother. Five years of fighting, I supposed that's what happened when someone blew the whistle in their workplace.

—

Nothing's changed. Peggy Reid, my ancestor on my mother's side, was the thirty-fourth Aboriginal child stolen from her family and culture. At the age of eight, Peggy was relocated into the first Parramatta Native Institute, three days after Christmas 1820. She was from the Burramattagal clan of the Dharug Nation in Sydney. The 'intake' number of my ancestor became her name for the first month of institutionalisation. Her identity was stripped immediately, and she was only known as Number 34 until given the name Peggy Reid.

—

I found my way through a rabbit warren of corridors that converged then separated into partitioned, box-like rooms divided by cafe-style booths. I found my solicitor. 'Hey, great to see you. We're in here. Let's get comfortable.' I sat at the long eight-seat table, walls of beige surrounding it.

If our people and culture had been celebrated here, our children would not have been stolen from their cultural and ancestral connections, language, family and Country. Our children are our hope and future. Without them, we aren't.

The proceedings began with an introduction to the State's legal representatives. Good cop – smiling with encouraging head nods. Lousy cop – colourless, cold eyes with a face to match.

I'd felt like my ancestor Peggy throughout the years. I became a number when I blew the whistle.

I listened to Peggy while I waited. They've done their best to break us, but it's never going to happen. Always Was, Always Will Be. That's what all the mobs say these days. Stitch them up and get out. Peggy sewed exquisite needlework. I could hear Mum too, 'Relax Dizzy, they couldn't organise a root in a brothel if they tried.'

———

I could see Harry the Greek's cafe in Lismore. It was always crowded. Red bench seats, thick toasted bread instead of bun hamburgers, and icy-cold caramel malted milkshakes served in the big silver container it was whipped in. Mum always said the caramel malted was the best. It still is. Everyone loved Harry.

Lismore welcomed its first Chinese family and restaurant. They were our neighbours and friends. We played in the restaurant's backyard; their mum would bring us crispy hot chips with zigzag sides, in a bowl, not newspaper. My six-year-old eyes gawked in awe, Chinese food! It was the most exotic food I'd ever seen or tasted. I didn't know what the stuff inside was, it was fluffy and white, encased in a crunch. Everyone seemed to love the Chinese family too.

We were allowed to talk to Harry the Greek and the Chinese family even though they looked different to us. Plus, they lived inside the township of Lismore. It was different for the black people; we were told to 'just walk past those black bastards'. Aboriginal people were shunned by everyone, it was like they belonged nowhere.

We moved to Rooty Hill in the 1970s. Our next-door neighbours were Harold, a tall, white-haired Englishman, and his Greek wife, Thelma. Their three children were black. Black children didn't have black parents. The black children I'd known and played with all had white parents.

—

A female go-between appeared. She carried scrap-sized pieces of paper, carefully folded origami-style, to the State. I sat watching the proceedings, present yet separate. As a child, I wondered why the black people lived where no-one could see them, on the outskirts. My child's head did not process the magnitude of what I saw. I watched and waited each afternoon for Peter and Paul to walk out of town on the road to nowhere, like the other coloured people. I didn't see them or any of the black children with white parents walk it. I didn't know then what I do now. Were they like the eight-month-old bub involved in my case, removed from their parents, culture and ancestors for questionable reasons?

How did the Traditional Owners of Australia become the most vilified people and culture in their own country, reduced to life without their biological parents on the fringes, in a land of diversity?

It was thirty years before I learnt of my Aboriginality. A party load of internal 'black bitches' released with unbridled joy. They loved life once they were out. Other revelations emerged. My father's ancestors were Elizabeth and William Shelly. In 1814, Governor Macquarie acted on the advice of Bill to establish the Parramatta Native Institution. The intent: Christianise, educate and civilise Aboriginal children. My dad's ancestors were directly responsible for the institutionalisation of my mum's ancestors. Conflict of interest or what! A domino effect that knocked down generation after generation.

Five years of a mustered life was completed in one hour of mediation. I wasted no time leaving. Mum would've said I ran out as quick as a rat up a drainpipe. Lobby found and exited. Air light, and sun hot, bright and delicious. Opening, cleansing and blessing. I needed it. I felt like a bin full of shit – a very sleek gold one with a real flash remote-controlled lid – but still a container of shit. I had wished for everything as a child. Mum, a wise woman, always told me, 'Wish in one hand and shit in another and see which one gets full first.' The bin, a clear indicator.

Do they see us as outsiders? Relegated to the outskirts, oppressed, ostracised and, from 1814 to the present, the word 'protection' used to steal our children from families and culture. Man, that's persistence! Two hundred years of attempting to destroy us, conditioning us all to believe we're a danger to ourselves and our children. Regulated decisions from the outset to ensure that we as a people lost sight of ourselves, our family and culture. How can the diversity of Australia's Traditional Owners' culture be fully active, acknowledged and respected while there is a systematic determination to destroy it?

I attempted to make sense of my memories, thoughts and feelings about this country that had always denied a home for the Traditional Owners. Is our culture perceived as 'one and belonging' to this country; do we have a place within its home and, if so, where?

Memories of growing up in a diverse Australia in the '60s, black but not yet knowing it, merged seamlessly with Australia now. There were more colours, more cultures, than ever. Me – my people, and my ancestors – just outsiders looking in.

SENSE OF BELONGING

COURTNEY THESEIRA

So let's lay it out there.

Female. Brown. Bisexual. Millennial. Tertiary-educated. Daughter of an Aboriginal and an immigrant from Malaysia.

I can say with a fair amount of certainty that there is always something about me that will annoy someone. If you happen to glance at the internet, I'm sure you'll realise that too.

It's also incredibly difficult not to take it personally. But I do try.

When diving into my life, I can't pinpoint the exact moment I discovered it wasn't always going to be sunshine. There were just a few tiny moments that built into something bigger. Passing comments that whittled away at self-esteem, actions from individuals that taught me to hunch my shoulders, and realisations in classrooms that my family tree will always be smaller than others.

When I was younger, I never had to search far to find a face like mine. I saw it every day in my little sister. When I moved to school, I saw it in my best friend, who had a similar heritage to mine except her father or mother was from the Philippines. Still, I knew I looked different to some. I had been jealous, as every child was, of the girl with the long blonde hair and sharp blue eyes. What I would have given for dead-straight hair instead of my wavy nest. I hated brushing my hair, if I'm honest. But I never saw my looks as an issue.

Other people did.

I remember when I was young not understanding how some of my older cousins had what my mother and father described as chips on their shoulders. But that is how the chips form. There's a moment when you start to realise that you aren't like everyone else. Then others make sure you know.

My father came home from work one day seething and upset. Someone on the street had yelled from a car that he should 'go back to his country'. But my father wasn't upset with them, he seemed mad at himself because he yelled back. He swore, called them names and his first thought was 'I shouldn't have done that'.

This struck me then and it stays with me now. Don't give them the satisfaction. It is not worth the pain, they are not worth the pain. But then I was fourteen. I had my first job at a fast-food restaurant, as most teenagers do. The place was small, and it always reeked of oil and stale bread. I stood at the front counter, my manager by my side as a man demanded that someone else serve him as I was not allowed.

I'll remember that sentence for the rest of my life.

'I don't want to be served by someone like her.'

I teach fourteen-year-olds now. That's my job. I watch their personalities forming, and attitudes growing. They want to be adults but they are still kids as well. They are losing and finding themselves again in mere seconds, being shaped by the world around them.

That's what makes me realise. I was a kid. One who had got her first kiss that year at a birthday party. One who really wanted to be an engineer, played the flute and thought a hundred dollars was the epitome of being rich.

One who didn't understand why this man hated her and who cried in the car before her next shift. I sobbed that day telling my father that I wished that I were white. He admitted to me later that he felt so much guilt because it was his colour that made me the colour I am today. He didn't know what to say.

I didn't give the man the satisfaction of seeing that reaction. I left the front counter and the manager served him.

The boys at the back refused to make his food.

At the time, I didn't think anything of it. Now I wish I could thank them. They could not have been older than sixteen. They were young but they knew then what I know now. It wasn't okay and it shouldn't have happened.

I brushed it off, as I brushed off the incidents that followed later in my life. You accept in this country that this is going to happen. If you don't, that's another chip.

People might read this and focus on the two boys at the back of the restaurant who took a stand. That's Australian. That's change. That's hope.

But I ask you to focus on the man for a moment. That man who saw a child and thought that I deserved that treatment. The grown-up who destroyed a teenager because he thought he had the right to. Is he the outlier? Is he the rare occurrence?

There are many reasons I say no.

However, I'm not saying that this type of behaviour only occurs on one side. This is the difficult part to swallow or even admit to myself.

I don't know my people. Being Aboriginal, to me, has been something I've been told, something that some members of my family don't admit, and something that hasn't been completely tangible or real. I don't know where I belong in a place that is meant to be my country and my home. I've had Elders hold my hands, tell me that I am one of them. I've had men, women, children smile at me like they know me. But I don't know them and I don't know where to begin to learn. No-one in my family truly knows who our people are, it is a piece of our history lost because of two generations taken.

Which is why I got called white in a room full of people that I thought I'd be accepted by. It hurt, I will be honest. It also became very obvious that I didn't belong.

That's the clear thing. I don't know where I belong. In all of my writings, art, poetry, in all the things I've poured my heart into, it has always been a clear theme. I write about the sense of belonging and what that would feel like. I think that's the only way I've truly experienced it.

People talk about the White Australia policy like it didn't work, and in some ways it didn't. But when I look at myself, I'm scared that it did. There's so much I don't know. Growing up, I was told that I am Aboriginal, but I don't know that I deserve to be one yet.

ABOUT THE AUTHORS

ALANA HICKS is a Papua New Guinean–Australian writer and director. Alana has long developed work informed by her connection to PNG, including the story *Smoke and Fire*, published by *Going Down Swinging*. Alana is forging a path as an emerging director, and is passionate about bringing Pasifika perspectives to a global audience. Her AACTA-nominated short film *Chicken* featured in the 2020 Flickerfest International Short Film Festival, for which she received the award for Best Direction in an Australian Short Film. She enjoys performing fairly obvious magic tricks in her downtime.

AMER ETRI is an educator who has worked predominantly in schools across Western Sydney over the past twenty years, teaching English, creative writing and history. He enjoys writing, especially poetry, and has performed spoken word poetry as a guest speaker at functions and as a participant in slam poetry competitions. His writing focuses mainly on self-expression, celebrating diversity, social justice and current political issues. Currently, he is involved in the production of a documentary series titled *Before 1770*, which details the interaction between Indonesian sailors and Indigenous Australians in northern Australia prior to European settlement.

AMY DUONG grew up in Melbourne but is now based in Canberra. She works as a data analyst and writes fiction and creative non-fiction in her spare time. She is a contributor to SBS Voices and has written about identity and Vietnamese–Australian culture. She is the daughter of refugees.

BON-WAI CHOU's stories have been awarded by *Glimmer Train* and Writer's Digest, published in *Southerly, Meanjin, The Age* and *Australian Short Stories*, and anthologised in *Growing up Asian in Australia*, among others. She is the recipient of an Australian Society of Authors 2020 Award Mentorship for Adult Fiction. Born in Chicago, she grew up in Hong Kong and Australia, and lives in Melbourne.

CAITLYN DAVIES-PLUMMER is a proud Aboriginal woman with family ties to the Barkindji language group. Caitlyn resides and works on Kaurna Country in Adelaide, South Australia, and is currently completing her Master of Clinical Psychology at the University of Adelaide. Working as an Aboriginal youth worker and counsellor, Caitlyn believes in having open and honest conversations about mental health. Caitlyn is also a passionate artist and enjoys singing in her spare time.

DR CHER COAD was born in Inner Mongolia and educated at the Central Drama Academy, Beijing. She has worked as a ringmaster with the Great Moscow Circus and as an actor, film director and producer, journalist and model. In 2012, Cher completed a PhD at Griffith University on international film co-productions. Nowadays, she balances a career as a real estate agent with a creative practice that spans writing, painting and theatre directing, while continuing to pursue scholarly research on intercultural topics. Cher lives in Melbourne with her partner, two teenage children, two dogs and a rabbit named Rabbit Downey Jnr.

COURTNEY THESEIRA is a Ngarrindjeri woman who grew up all around Australia, living in Perth, Canberra and Adelaide. She is now residing in Melbourne to study her Masters in Student Wellbeing. As a history and English teacher, Courtney knows the importance of representation and stories being told. It is a passion of hers to write stories that future generations can read, relate to and learn from. When she is not writing, Courtney enjoys gaming, painting, and trying to convince herself that loving coffee is a solid personality trait.

DIANNE USSHER is a proud Dharug woman, born in the Blue Mountains and raised in northern New South Wales until her family moved to Western Sydney. Dianne has since returned to live in the Blue Mountains, the country of her Dharug ancestors. Dianne is a First Nations storyteller and artist. Her work is motivated by the need for social change for the Traditional Owners of Australia. Dianne is passionate about her people, culture, survival and storytelling truth. Dianne's faith in the unity of her Dharug, Jewish and Christian ancestral connections and her strong sense of Spirit, community and love of Country inspire her work.

ESMÉ JAMES is a PhD candidate at the University of Melbourne. She has published two novels, *Honeyflower and Pansy* (2014) and *The Awakening* (2017), and has also produced a range of poetry, short stories and non-fiction articles for publications such as *Hecate*, *Archer*, *Farrago* and *Lot's Wife*. Esmé was the recipient of the University of Melbourne's Shakespeare and Fay Marles scholarships in 2019. In 2020, she was listed in the Top 30 Emerging Writers by SBS Australia. Esmé is also known for her irreverent lecture series on TikTok.

HUGH JORGENSEN is a bureaucrat with a dictionary. He wrote his entry for this anthology inside a hotel shaped like a crocodile.

JACKIE BAILEY is a professional writer, researcher and recognised international expert on cultural diversity in the arts. Jackie is also an ordained interfaith minister, deathwalker and a practising funeral celebrant. Her autofiction manuscript was shortlisted for the KYD Unpublished Manuscript Award 2018, and long-listed for The Wheeler Centre's Next Chapter Award 2019. Jackie is an alumna of Varuna: The National Writers House, and has written for various collections and publications. She has a Creative Writing PhD from UNSW. Jackie is currently working on a non-fiction book about spirituality for non-religious people.

JASON PHU is a practising artist whose artworks explore Chinese histories in Australia, his own family history and Chinese/Vietnamese folktales. He was born in Sydney and is now based in Melbourne, where he enjoys writing poetry and short stories.

KARLA HART is an award-winning filmmaker, writer, director, producer, Noongar dancer, singer and actor. She completed her Bachelor of Arts, majoring in contemporary performance, at Edith Cowan University and has a Certificate IV in Aboriginal Theatre from the West Australian Academy of Performing Arts. Karla is passionate about her Noongar heritage, in particular language and stories.

KAYE COOPER has been smitten with language from a young age. She believes that words have power. They can destroy or build up. They can have colour, rhythm, texture and weight. Words can evoke strong emotions and give flight to our imaginings. Kaye has endeavoured to impart this love of language to those she has taught throughout her long career as an educator. She is looking forward to learning more about the craft of writing and to her next chapter in life as an author.

LAL PERERA arrived in Perth as a three-year-old and since then has spent a lot of time wondering, talking and writing about life as a migrant in Australia. Lal's work has appeared in *Meanjin*, *Westerly* and other Australian publications.

MAHA SIDAOUI has been writing for more than thirty years: first letters, then lyrics and later stories. Maha has a love for words and writes in order to search her childhood and early years for whatever it was that made her the person and writer that she has become. Maha's screenplay, One Arabian Night, was shortlisted in the Big Break Screenwriting Contest, and in 2015 her fiction work was shortlisted for the Deborah Cass Prize. Her short story

'Choices' appeared in a 2016 RMIT anthology and can be heard on the Memoria podcast. She is currently working on her debut YA novel, *One Arabian Girl*.

MARGARITA D'HEUREUX migrated to Australia with her parents and brother when she was fourteen, following her older siblings who had arrived in the late 1960s and early 1970s. Margarita is an avid reader with a passion for murder mysteries. She also dabbles in oil and pastel painting, mostly landscapes and the odd portrait. Edgar Degas is one of her greatest influences. Margarita has written short stories based around her childhood and has created a compilation of traditional recipes from Trinidad.

MICHAEL SUN is a writer, designer and broadcaster based on Gadigal land, Sydney who loves beautiful dogs and ugly fonts. His work, which revolves around the intersections between queerness, technology and memory, has been published in *The Guardian Australia*, *The Monthly*, *ABC Arts*, *VICE*, *The Age*, *The Sydney Morning Herald*, and many more. In his spare time, he gasbags on FBi Radio. His story 'Just Dance' was first performed at Queerstories.

MIRANDA JAKICH, born to immigrant parents, only realised on her first day of school that the other kids spoke a language called English. Strangely, none of these kids understood the importance of Yugoslavia and Tito Nostalgia. Her quest to learn English and fit in led to a university education, then a series of jobs where words always mattered. 'Fish people' is her first published work after a lifetime of sharing stories only with her friends.

MONIKKA ELIAH is an Assyrian–Australian writer from Fairfield. She is a member of Sweatshop: Western Sydney Literacy Movement. Her work has been published in *The Big Black Thing*, *SBS Voices*, *Sweatshop Women*, *Runway Journal*, *Southerly*, *Kill Your Darlings* and *The Lifted Brow*. She received a Southlands Breakthrough Award in 2018 and a Wheeler Centre Playwright Hot Desk Fellowship in 2020. She has presented work at the NSW Writers' Centre, Wollongong Writers Festival, Sydney Writers' Festival, NYW Festival, National Play Festival, WITS Festival Fatale, STC Rough Draft and Sydney Festival. She is currently developing her debut novel as a recipient of an Australia Council Resilience Fund grant.

NADIA JOHANSEN is a Gungarri writer and poet from Mitchell in south-west Queensland who is living and writing on unceded Turrbal/Yuggera land in Brisbane. She is studying a Bachelor of Fine Arts in Creative Writing at Queensland University of Technology. She works as an editor intern at *black&write!*, which allows her to share the magic, power and resilience of First Nations writing with the world. Nadia believes storytelling is essential to how we conceive of ourselves as individuals and as communities, and that by changing those stories we can change our societies.

NAEUN KIM hails from the colourful Sydney suburb of Punchbowl, hence her love for Lebanese food and the Canterbury Bulldogs. She blames her mum for her addiction to storytelling thanks to all the books that kept her company as an only, but never lonely, child. She is an overt Francophile and a sucker for puns and dad jokes, which can be a pun-ishment for her friends. Born in Australia to Korean parents, Naeun disappointed them by shunning maths, instead insisting on a career in nosiness (journalism). She currently works as a news producer and hopes her parents are finally proud – despite featuring heavily in her story.

NAKUL LEGHA was born in India and grew up in Bhutan, where television was banned. Now he's making up for lost time by spending most of his days watching and working in television. He cares about hearing and telling new kinds of Australian stories, and can be found loitering around the Netflix Australia offices helping to make this happen. He has previously worked as a media lawyer and for the ABC (where he was officially B1 in Bananas in Pyjamas for one day).

PRATEETI SABHLOK started learning synchronised swimming just before her tenth birthday, after getting bored with normal swimming. Since then she has been involved in the sport at a national level and founded a synchronised swimming club in Melbourne. Prateeti has won awards from the Maroondah and Moreland city councils and received the Victorian Premier's Volunteer Champions Impact Award for her work in synchronised swimming. Outside of sport, Prateeti works full-time and enjoys being creative.

ROSIE OFORI WARD is a Ghanaian–English–Australian freelance writer and literary critic based in Naarm/Melbourne. Her writing has appeared in publications including *Salty*, *Djed Press* and *Ramona Mag*. She is passionate about the politics of identity, social policy and intersectional feminism. She writes so that one day, young brown girls like her will be able to find themselves in literature.

SAM PRICE is a professional film and TV producer and editor, having worked for some of Australia's major broadcasters and production companies as well as digital marketing agencies. Throughout high school and university, Sam was part of multiple writing clubs and film societies, and spent her downtime crafting poetry, short stories and experimental pieces of work. Obsessed with story, Sam used her lull in work during the COVID pandemic as an opportunity to delve back into writing. In all her work she focuses on championing and promoting stories of diversity genuinely and authentically.

SERPIL SENELMIS is the co-founder of Written & Recorded, an agency specialising in podcast production, copywriting and communications training. She has worked across Australia's mainstream media in newspapers, radio, TV and online for more than twenty years. She was the first Turkish–Australian to host shows on commercial radio, the ABC and Channel 9. Coming from a strong tradition of storytelling, she has loved crafting narratives from the moment her tiny fingers could grasp a pen. Serpil holds a Bachelor of Arts (English and Media) from Edith Cowan University, and an Associate Degree in Broadcasting from the West Australian Academy of Performing Arts.

SITA WALKER is a high-school teacher of English and literature who writes true stories and poetry. Coming from sheep farmers, gardeners, pastors, shopkeepers and teachers, she loves a good yarn and anyone with an honest appreciation of what it means to be human. Sita grew up in Toowoomba, but now lives in Brisbane with her three children, a doting dog and a cat that disapproves.

TANIA OGIER was born and raised in Melbourne, though Brisbane has been the sunny setting for recent chapters of her life. She has also lived in Papua New Guinea and Scotland, and has a son who was born in Glasgow. Tania currently works in the education sector. She holds an Honours Degree in English Language Studies with Literature, and for four years was a contributing arts writer for *The Garb Wire*. Her favourite genre is bildungsroman, the sentimental sap in her adoring a heart-wrenching coming-of-age tale.

TRENT WALLACE grew up on Darkinjung Country before moving to Gadigal Country to pursue his legal career. Trent is a law lecturer and a First Nations advisor and lawyer in a top-tier global law firm. In each role he has held, Trent has been either the first or first and only Aboriginal person, and seeks to lay a strong foundation for other mob to come through the legal profession. Having recently moved to Meanjin Country, Trent is seeking out brunch spots – brunch is a sport to him. Trent dedicates this story to his Osbourne-esque family. Long live the rebel hearts of the world!